# THINKING COP
# FEELING COP

## A Study In Police Personalities

Center for Applications of Psychological Type, Inc.
Gainesville, Florida

Copyright 1999 Stephen M. Hennessy

All rights reserved. No part of this book, except as specifically noted below, may be reproduced in any form or by any electronic or mechanical means including information storage retrieval systems without permission in writing from the publisher (CAPT). Exception: A reviewer may quote brief passages in a review.

Published by
Center for Applications of Psychological Type, Inc.
2815 N.W. 13th Street, Suite 401
Gainesville, FL 32609
(352) 375-0150 • (800) 777-2278

CAPT, the CAPT logo, and Center for Applications of Psychological Type are trademarks of Center for Applications of Psychological Type, Inc., Gainesville, FL.

Myers-Briggs Type Indicator and MBTI are registered trademarks of Consulting Psychologists Press, Inc., Palo Alto, CA.

Printed in the United States of America.

First edition 1992
Second edition 1995
Third edition 1999

ISBN 0-935652-45-0

Library of Congress Cataloging-in-Publication Data

Hennessy, Stephen M.
    Thinking cop, feeling cop: a study in police personalities/ Stephen M. Hennessy. -- 3rd ed.
       p. cm.
    Includes bibliographical references.
    ISBN 0-935652-45-0
    1. Personality and occupation. 2. Myers-Briggs Type Indicator.
3. Law enforcement --Psychological aspects. 4. Police psychology.
I. Title.
BF698.9.O3H46   1998
363.2'01'9--dc21

98-43256
CIP

# Acknowledgements

As the case with anyone writing about the MBTI, or any psychological type for that matter, profound appreciation must be expressed for the work and wisdom of Katharine C. Briggs and Isabel Briggs Myers, in bringing Carl Jung's theory to life, along with the numerous scholars and practitioners who have, through their research with the MBTI, helped make some sense of the complexity of trying to understand each other.

Appreciation must also be expressed for Dr. Mary H. McCaulley, Gerald P. Macdaid, and the many professionals for their diligent work with the Center for Applications of Psychological Type located in Gainesville, Florida. The non-profit Center was established in 1975 to offer a variety of services to further the understanding of psychological type. Among its many functions, CAPT serves as a central repository for data collected through the use of the MBTI which is analyzed for type differences in occupations, age, and educational levels. The statistics from several occupations compared to the data discussed in this book from the law enforcement profession were obtained from that data bank. I am indebted to the Center and those professionals. I urge those of you using the MBTI in the criminal justice area to share your findings with CAPT. The information the Center has reflecting our occupation will serve to deepen our understanding of the men and women in our profession and assist us in meeting the challenges of the future.

My thanks goes also to two people at the Center for Applications of Psychological Type who were instrumental in the publication of this third edition: Margaret Fields, who handled the production of the book, Jamelyn Johnson, who proofed and edited the manuscript, and Stephanie Hencin who proofed and edited the format.

I would like to express my personal appreciation to the many police executives who willingly gave of their time to contribute to the contents of this book. Of those, I would like to specifically thank my good friend and professional colleague Thomas L. Reding, a Commander with the St. Paul, Minnesota Police Department, for his intellect and insight. Hobart M. Henson, Director of the National Center for State, Local and International Training, Federal Law Enforcement Academy, Glynco, Georgia, was the mentor who introduced me to the MBTI and to other issues on leadership, which ultimately made this book and its previous two editions possible. I also appreciate the interest and comments on my work by William L. Tafoya, Ph.D., the Director of Research and Planning, Office of International Criminal Justice, The University of Chicago, and an internationally recognized expert on the future of policing.

I appreciate the countless opportunities that my colleagues at the Phoenix, Arizona Police Department have afforded me as their Training Advisor to continue looking into the ramifications that cognitive styles have on our profession. I am especially appreciative of the support of Division Director Gerald Richard, II, Esq., as well as Training Bureau Commanders Donald Swanson and John L. Buchanan. This is an outstanding police agency under the professional and very capable leadership of Police Chief Harold Hurtt.

# Table of Contents

|  | PREFACE . . . . . . . . . . . . . . . . . . . . . . . . . . . . . . . . . . . vii |
|---|---|
|  | INTRODUCTION . . . . . . . . . . . . . . . . . . . . . . . . . . . . . x |
| 1 | UNDERSTANDING CARL JUNG'S THEORY . . . . . . . . . 1 |
| 2 | THE LAW ENFORCEMENT PROFESSION . . . . . . . . . . . . 8 |
| 3 | THE PERSONALITY TYPES IN POLICING . . . . . . . . . . . 13 |
| 4 | DIFFERENCES IN COMMUNICATION . . . . . . . . . . . . . . 23 |
| 5 | CHOOSING LAW ENFORCEMENT AS A PROFESSION . . . . . . . . . . . . . . . . . . . . . . . . . . . . . . 35 |
| 6 | MANAGEMENT STYLES AND HOW THEY MAY DIFFER . . . . . . . . . . . . . . . . . . . . . . . . 43 |
| 7 | FEELING TYPES AND HOW THEY DIFFER . . . . . . . . . . . 53 |
| 8 | WOMEN IN LAW ENFORCEMENT . . . . . . . . . . . . . . . . 63 |
| 9 | POSSIBLE WEAKNESSES OF EACH STYLE . . . . . . . . . . . 68 |
| 10 | POLICE CONFLICTS WITH OTHER PROFESSIONS . . . 77 |
| 11 | BENEFITS OF UNDERSTANDING DIFFERENCES OF PERSONALITY IN POLICING . . . . 84 |
| 12 | WATCHING TYPE AT WORK . . . . . . . . . . . . . . . . . . . . . . 93 |

**13** COGNITIVE STYLES OF POLICE AND THE
CHANGING CULTURAL COMMUNITY ........................101

**14** COGNITIVE STYLES AND TEACHING IN
THE LAW ENFORCEMENT PROFESSION .....................110

**APPENDICES**

A - THE MYERS-BRIGGS TYPE INDICATOR .................125

B - POLICE PERSONALITY RESEARCH .........................134

C - PERSONALITY TYPES
IN OTHER PROFESSIONS .........................................138

**REFERENCES** ....................................................................146

**ABOUT THE AUTHOR** ....................................................149

# Preface

Many years ago, I had an opportunity to attend one of Steve Hennessy's leadership classes, which had become the regional management classes to attend if you wanted to learn something. In one of the courses we were divided into groups of five where we worked together for one intense week on leadership techniques. I was fascinated that the group seemed to work exceptionally well together. Each participant's strengths and weaknesses seemed to be balanced by those of other group members as we worked through complex leadership strategies. After the class we all commented on the fact we had all worked so well together, and Steve told us he had used the Myers-Briggs Type Indicator to assist in making up the groups. He had placed differing cognitive styles together to bring a variety of strengths into play as we worked with our problem scenarios. He believed that one primary reason we functioned so well together was that these differing abilities complemented each other during our discussions.

With this concrete example of the usefulness of the Myers-Briggs Type Indicator, I became a believer and a student of the Indicator. Finally, I was able to better understand why my chief functioned as he did, and why the quickest way to lose his interest was to bury him with the details of a project. I was able to understand why, as a young patrol officer teamed up with an older veteran whose style of operating was so vastly different from mine, our strengths seemed to compliment each other so that we functioned very effectively as a team.

The understanding you can gain from this book will help put these and other internal personnel issues into a new and different perspective. It can also assist the profession in understanding some of the natural conflict in communication we often have with the diverse communities that we serve.

I truly believe this book is an important addition to every police executive's knowledge base. We all need every tool we can possibly lay our hands on as the role of leadership becomes more and more complex.

Read this book for enjoyment. It's easy to get through. You will recognize situations we all see in our lives as law enforcement officers. Many of them are humorous and some of them are sad. Look at it hard, though, a second time for a new understanding of how people function that will assist you in dealing with others in your personal life and professional career.

Thomas L. Reding, Esq., Commander
St. Paul Police Department
St. Paul, Minnesota
Past President-Society of Police Futurists International

---

Since the mid-1970s, two writing styles have predominated in discussions of police psychology, cognitive style and personality assessment. The literature has tended to be either excessively academic or exceedingly mundane. This is, in part, why police administrators make such little use of Carl Jung's conceptual framework of cognitive styles or the Myers-Briggs Type Indicator. Effectively explaining the complex nature of opposing psychological poles or the characteristics that distinguish perception and judgment combinations is not easy. If the explanations are oversimplified, scholars quickly become bored, while practitioners believe they are being patronized and insufficiently informed to make applications of this important research.

It is little wonder then that authors have struggled with determining how best to present this important field of behavioral sciences. The author has managed to avoid these pitfalls and to bridge the gap between theory and the "real world." Subsequently, this book neither insults the intelligence of scholars nor ignores the needs of practitioners.

The turbulent environment in which law enforcement currently operates draws close scrutiny and occasionally shrill criticism from the far right, the far left, and the political center. This makes it essential for field training officers, first-line supervisors, middle managers, administrators, and academy directors, as well as college and university faculty members, to develop a clear understanding of the various ways law enforcement officers assess the problems that they confront on a daily basis. Of equal importance is learning to recognize the internal "drivers" that motivate individuals. In short, leaders must be cognizant of their subordinates' cognitive preferences in order to draw more fully on their strengths.

*Thinking Cop, Feeling Cop* provides insight into why officers who usually perform brilliantly may fail in certain circumstances. The book also sheds a great deal of light on the law enforcement profession and its interactions with the various diverse communities it serves. It is a very manageable book that presents rather complex material in a clear and concise manner. It is an exceptional presentation that would benefit any law enforcement administrator.

William L. Tafoya, Ph.D.
Director, Research and Training
Office of International Criminal Justice
University of Illinois at Chicago
Founder - Society of Police Futurists International

# Introduction

Law enforcement systems occupy a unique position in our society. They represent a source of power that is not readily understood by many individuals. Agencies play a critical and necessary role in the preservation of public safety, maintaining public order, and enforcing the law. Police officers have often been the target of widespread complaint and criticism, particularly in recent years. Police officers have been characterized as being cold, condescending, matter-of-fact, and without compassion. They often seem to be at odds with the news media, social workers, and other helping professions. As our cities continue to become much more diverse, the conflict in communication with the various communities we serve is becoming an important issue.

As law enforcement executives realize, a law enforcement agency's most important asset is its employees. Agency leaders have a clear need to understand how their employees function on the job, and how they work best while involved with the many tasks of policing.

Recruiting individuals for job functions related to policing is a continual challenge. Intelligence, job interest, and physical agility tests, as well as personal interviews, are all used in various combinations. Recruiting efforts, however, may still target the wrong individuals for the job, or an individual may enter a profession and later realize that it was not the job they believed it to be. In addition to recruiting, the functions of training and motivating police officers are critical. Police agencies have a responsibility to understand the reasons for lack of motivation, low productivity, transfer and attrition rates, and poor performance among police personnel.

As all police executives know, being a law enforcement manager immersed in the daily happenings of the profession offers a unique insight into how people function in the occupation. To facilitate communication and to point out differences in Perception and Judgment in team-building exercises, I have been using the Myers-Briggs Type Indicator with attendees in leadership classes and courses in developing cultural awareness. This inventory, based on Carl Jung's theories regarding personality type, helps people understand their preferred ways of taking in information and making decisions.

Knowing how individuals prefer to function in the profession can help police managers better understand the different ways their employees approach problems and the various strengths they use on a daily basis. This knowledge can be used to help understand why some police personnel function better in certain jobs than in others and why some officers may appear to be poorly suited for the occupation of policing. Insights can be gained into why police personnel look at crime and violators differently than many social workers, defense attorneys, representatives of the media, and psychologists. Additionally, it helps to gain insights on the police culture itself and interactions with diverse communities.

As a result of teaching numerous leadership classes and watching the on-the-job behavior of those police executives attending, the importance of understanding the ways we function best in the profession has become evident. I have spent over ten years conducting various studies on police personalities using the MBTI as a basis for categorizing the differences I observed. Looking at the results continues to open up a whole new dimension for better understanding the members of the law enforcement profession and their interactions among themselves and with the communities they serve.

Even though the Myers-Briggs Type Indicator was used in confirming various preferences in the way that people preferred to do things, it is not necessary for you to take the Indicator to understand the contents of this book. Differences and similarities of behavior in individuals are very evident and easily understood by watching other people and how they interact with their co-workers and perform their job functions. The important issue here is that there is a rational, understandable, reason why people behave in certain ways. Knowing this can give us all an excellent tool to perform better.

This third edition includes additional observations that I have made as the training administrator for a major city police department. These observations reinforce my conviction that the understanding of type in the law enforcement profession can only help to assist us as administrators in our leadership roles with our organizations and the communities we serve. The new material in this third edition includes communication styles, insights and information on course methodology, and how to successfully present various course materials to law enforcement professionals.

The study of law enforcement and how we prefer to function can help executives in the profession to better understand their personnel and can give those individuals outside the profession insights into why police perform as they do. For the cop on the beat, understanding different ways their co-workers and others prefer to take in information and make decisions can help them deal with those differences better.

This book is written for police executives, the officer on the street, representatives of the media, and other individuals involved in the various fields of civil and criminal justice. Because of the varied backgrounds of those who wish to expand their knowledge on police personality, the book has many facets. To the police administrators, the chapter on the police profession will be elementary and simplistic. It has been included to re-draft what the occupation is really about from a lay person's point of view. The chapter on Jung's theory may be complex to some, but is helpful in understanding how he categorized the characteristics of individuals and the different ways they communicate.

I have included several appendices for those who may wish to read more detailed information on the Myers-Briggs Type Indicator, more complex police personality research, and research in other professions. In your reading, I hope you will enjoy some of the insights this book has to offer about the ways we deal with one another.

# 1 Understanding Carl Jung's Theory

Carl G. Jung, a Swiss physician and psychologist, was a contemporary and associate of Alfred Adler and Sigmund Freud during the late eighteen hundreds. Jung observed great disagreements between Freud and Adler, who were eminent psychologists and researchers of their day, in their understanding of how people used their thought processes. The actual substance of the disagreements is really unimportant here; however Jung, in examining the two points of view of both Adler and Freud, found them to reflect attractively simple differences in the way each looked at things. As complex as individual personalities are, he considered these patterns to be an extremely interesting phenomenon.

He found it interesting that two people from the same basic background and environment could approach an issue from two completely different points of view, when current scientific thought generally held that personality was much more of a product of environment than inheritance. Contrary to the thinking of the day, Jung felt that a person's psychological type primarily was a product of genetic factors and that at birth or shortly thereafter, the determinant of the way a person preferred to function in the world was formed. To this day, scientists and psychologists still debate the issue of whether "nature," which would mean inherited characteristics, or "nurture," meaning the forces of the present environment, has more to do with the development of personality. You would assume that it is a combination of both factors that shape the personality of an individual. However, an interesting thought about the important effect genes may have in personality development may lie in a question you could ask a mother of two children born nine months apart, same sex, with the same father and mother, same environment, with the same socio-economic factors. If asked, she will usually comment about her innate feeling that both children are completely different from each other, and this, only days after birth of the second child.

## The Four Functions: Mental Processing

In 1921 Jung wrote a book called *Psychological Types* that explained his theory. Jung identified four basic functions which serve as a structure for an individual's personality, two involved in taking in of information, or Perception, and two involving decision making, or Judgment.

He believed people take in information in two ways, through Sensing or through Intuition. These he called the Perceiving functions. According to Jung, people naturally have a preference for one way of taking in information over the other. After accessing this information, a decision must be made or a conclusion reached. This is accomplished through one of two processes, Thinking or Feeling. Jung referred to these as the two Judging functions. Jung felt these functions were an integral part of a person's personality which resulted in certain patterns of behavior which could be classified. The possible combinations of Perception and Judgment, according to Jung, were Sensing with Thinking (ST), Sensing with Feeling (SF), Intuition with Thinking (NT), and Intuition with Feeling (NF).

## The Perceptive Functions: Sensing or Intuition

In Jung's system, individuals experience the world through their Perceptive function. This is the taking in of information either by Sensing or Intuition.

**Sensing types (S)** use Sensing and Intuition, but prefer and develop the use of Sensing as the stronger and preferred function. Sensing types gain information through sight, sound, taste, smell, and touch. People preferring Sensing generally see only what exists at the immediate time. Strengths usually associated with this function are practicality, being very realistic, being grounded in the present with a great aptitude for detail. In careers, higher Sensing scores correlate with engineers, bankers, accountants, those in various hands-on trades, and those professions requiring a close attention to detail.

**Intuitive types (N)** on the other hand, use both Sensing and Intuition, but prefer Intuition, seeing things in a more generalized, global way. The person who is using this function is less aware of specific details, but sees abstract patterns and relationships. Strengths usually associated with Intuition are creativity, global thinking, planning and research skills, and being able to see patterns and relationships. In careers, higher Intuition scores correlate with psychologists, artists, reporters, university educators, and those professions calling for abstractions and patterns or symbols.

The preference for the use of one over the other can be visualized as being on a continuum, with Sensing at one end and Intuition on the other. When we are taking in information we are using the processes of Sensing or Intuition. We are using one **or** the other at a time, though, not both simultaneously.

Jung felt that the preference for one over the other was "constitutional" or occurring at or near birth. One way to understand the preference issue better is for you to take a pen or pencil in your dominant hand, usually the right, and then sign your name. Then, transfer the pen or pencil to your other hand, usually the left, and write it again. You may groan and complain or laugh at the effort it takes and you may say you can't do it. Of course you can, even though it usually does not appear as well written as when your dominant hand was used. This little exercise can illustrate how inborn preferences become stronger with use and those less used, not as well developed. Jung stated that people have a preference for a particular way of perceiving, either through Sensing or Intuition. He said that when we use that preference over and over again, we become more familiar with that preference and more confident with its use. Most of us fall within the continuum, with one preference stronger than the other.

Typically, if people prefer the Intuitive function over the Sensing one, they concentrate on the total picture, but may tend to miss detail. On the other hand, if people perceive in specific detail, they tend to overlook the total picture.

## The Judgment Functions: Thinking or Feeling

Jung believed that the information acquired through Perception undergoes a "distillation" process through which an individual can make various decisions. As with taking in of information (Perception), Jung believed that people make decisions (Judgment) through one of two preferred functions, Thinking or Feeling, again, along a continuum.

Making a decision through Thinking means you decide about a matter in a very analytical and impersonal way without necessarily taking into consideration the impact on the people involved. **Thinking types (T)** use both Thinking and Feeling but prefer Thinking for making judgments. Strengths developed from the use of Thinking as a judgment preference include objectivity, impartiality, a sense of fairness and justice, and skill in applying logical analysis. In careers, higher Thinking scores correlate with engineering, math, business, technical fields, sciences, and hands-on trades.

**Feeling types (F)**, on the other hand, use both Thinking and Feeling, but prefer to reach judgments through Feeling. They tend to employ a process of reasoning which involves taking people into consideration first. Strengths typically associated with the use of Feeling as a judgment preference include an understanding of people, a desire for harmony, and a capacity for warmth, empathy, and compassion. In careers, higher Feeling scores correlate with social service, religious activities, teaching, and health care.

## The Dominant and Auxiliary Processes

To understand how the functions work with each other during our daily lives, we need to understand the way the Perceptive and Judgment functions work together. One function will be dominant, the other one the auxiliary process.

If the dominant process is a Judging one (Thinking or Feeling), the auxiliary process must be a Perceiving one (Sensing or Intuition). Likewise, if the dominant process is a Perceiving process, obviously the auxiliary needs to be a Judging one. As an example, if a person's dominant function is a Perceiving one of Intuition, the auxiliary function must be a Judging function of either Thinking or Feeling. Logically it cannot be another Perceiving function as the information has already been perceived though Intuition. Besides serving as a complement to the dominant process, the auxiliary serves as a balance between Extraversion and Introversion.

Some individuals may dislike the idea of one process being more dominant than the other and prefer to think of themselves as using all functions equally well. Jung thought, however, that such impartiality kept all of the functions relatively undeveloped and produced a "primitive mentality," because opposite ways of doing the same thing will interfere with each other if none has a priority.

## Extraversion and Introversion

Jung further theorized the existence of Introversion and Extraversion, which he called "attitudes." Extraverts typically focus on the outer world, while Introverts are more comfortable focusing on their inner world of thoughts and ideas. Because the main focus of this book is to look at the various ways officers differed in the ways they preferred to take in information and make decisions, I have not specifically mentioned the way Extraversion and Introversion play out in communication. However, during my interviews with officers, I kept Extraversion and Introversion in mind. For example, if people preferred Introversion, I would just wait as they internally formulated their answers. If they preferred Extraversion, I would banter back and forth with them until they arrived at a conclusion about an issue we were discussing. If you are interested in the attitudes of Introversion and Extraversion and Jung's theory, they are covered in more detail in Appendix A, dealing with the development of the Indicator.

## The Basis for Understanding This Book

As was stated earlier in this chapter, the two possible preferences a person could use in taking in and processing information (Perception) were either through one's five senses (Sensing) or through abstract patterns and relationships (Intuition). The two possible ways that a person could prefer to make decisions (Judgment) about a matter would be through either impersonal logic (Thinking) or personal evaluation of impact on people (Feeling).

The four combinations of those processes, which can be referred to as cognitive styles, are defined as follows:

| Perception | - | Judgment | Style |
|---|---|---|---|
| Sensing | - | Thinking | ST |
| Sensing | - | Feeling | SF |
| Intuitive | - | Feeling | NF |
| Intuition | - | Thinking | NT |

Each one of these combinations of cognitive styles is characterized by a variety of behaviors that a person demonstrates over a period of time. Myers called the ST combination practical and matter-of-fact, the NT combination logical and ingenious, the SF combination sympathetic and friendly, and the NF combination enthusiastic and insightful. Each one of us is an individual. However, since we share preferred ways of doing things with many others, we share certain common characteristics. These characteristics can be quantified and can help us do a much better job in relating to and understanding one another.

# 2 The Law Enforcement Profession

Police officers represent a fascinating anomaly in the United States. They are vested with an enormous amount of power and authority in a government founded under a system that generally dislikes and fears centralized power. The specific authority they possess to use force, detain, arrest, and search people can be awesome.

Yet, as a democracy, we are heavily dependent upon police to maintain the degree of order necessary to make a free society possible. Herman Goldstein, a scholar and police researcher, commented that police prevent people from preying on each other, provide a sense of security, facilitate movement, resolve conflicts, and protect the rights of free elections, free speech, and freedom of assembly on which the continuation of our free society depends. The strength of a democracy and the quality of life enjoyed by its citizens are determined in large measure by the ability of the police to discharge their duties. The average citizen thinks of police work as primarily concerned with preventing crime and apprehending criminals. When crime increases, or a particularly heinous crime is committed, the public usually calls for more or better police personnel. Conversely, when crime declines in a certain area, the police often get, or try to take, the credit.

The real job of policing is far different from some media portrayals in the newspapers, radio or on television. As stated by James Q. Wilson, a pragmatic, highly respected professor of government at Harvard, the majority of calls have little to do with crime and a lot to do with medical emergencies, family quarrels, neighborhood disputes, auto accidents, barking dogs, minor traffic violations, and similar events. Those calls that do involve actual felony crimes such as burglaries, robberies, and auto thefts, typically occur long after the event has taken place.

People today look on police more as crime fighters rather than guardians of the public's safety, because this is an era of violent crime. The headlines of any newspaper are full of stories of violence that occurred the night before in any city, not only in this country, but throughout the world. Because we live with instant communication, news of schoolyard shootings, criminal bombings and other acts of criminal violence and terrorism are broadcast throughout the United States immediately. For various reasons, including the continuing epidemics of crack cocaine and manufacturing of methamphetamine, crime in the United States has become increasingly more violent.

The flood of such news greatly heightens our awareness and concern about crime. We watch numerous television shows that show cops moving in nonstop action for sixty minutes at a time (with appropriate breaks for commercials). On television a police radio report is received over the air and the officers speed through the streets (red lights on and sirens screaming), come to a tire-screeching halt, bail out of the cruiser (usually while it is spinning on its top after a spectacular crash), chase a violator down an alley into a dead end and either square off into a fight or pull him down from a chain link fence.

The above poses an exciting and interesting plot line, but may be somewhat inaccurate. As for the recent phenomenon of video taped true life action police and rescue shows such as *Cops* and *True Stories of the Highway Patrol*, police are viewed as rolling from call to call in non-stop action on a daily basis. Much more action occurs in the larger cities than in the smaller jurisdictions, but most law enforcement officers from all departments get plenty of action. Somewhat differing from the media's non-stop action-filled portrayal of police work, Charles Saunders, another police researcher, compiled a lengthy list of attributes and skills a police officer must have to perform the job of policing. These include the ability to:

- Endure long periods of monotony during routine patrol, and yet react quickly and effectively to a problem situation on the street or to the radio dispatcher;
- Gain extensive knowledge of the patrol area, not only the physical characteristics, but the normal routine of events, and the usual behavior patterns of its residents;
- Exhibit initiative, problem solving capacity, effective judgment, and imagination in coping with numerous and varying situations involved in a daily tour: a family disturbance, a potential suicide, a robbery in progress, a traffic accident, a medical emergency, or a disaster (police officers refer to this as having a lot of "common" or "street" sense);
- Make prompt and effective decisions, sometimes having to do with life or death, and be able to evaluate a situation quickly and take appropriate action;
- Demonstrate mature judgment as to whether an arrest is warranted or not, whether to warn or let go, or be willing to take control and use any physical force necessary to control the situation;
- Demonstrate critical awareness in discerning signs of conditions that are not ordinary, or circumstances that may indicate a crime is in progress;
- Exhibit a number of complex psychomotor skills such as driving a vehicle in emergency situations, firing a weapon accurately under extreme and varied conditions, and maintaining agility, endurance and strength in taking an individual into custody while using the minimum force necessary;

- Exhibit a professional, self-assured presence and a self-confident manner in dealing with offenders, the public, and the courts;
- Be capable of restoring equilibrium to social groups such as mediating a family dispute, handling neighborhood problems, and dealing with street gangs;
- Maintain objectivity when working with a host of special interest groups such as the press, family, victims, and offenders; and,
- Maintain a balanced perspective in the face of exposure to the worst side of human nature.

## Tactical Necessity and Community Relations Approaches

These above descriptions are considered to be basic to the job of policing, regardless of the nature and size of the community policed. The reality of policing, however, offers an interesting and growing paradox, that of the need to be tactically aware and prepared for any violent event which calls for tactical units such as S.W.A.T. and bomb squads, as well as to continually pay attention to the needs of the community through other programs such as School Resource Programs, Gang Resistance and Education Programs, D.A.R.E., Community Awareness and Neighborhood Policing, and Bike Patrols.

William L. Tafoya, Ph.D., the founder of the Police Futurists Society International and a highly respected expert on the future of policing, predicted in his landmark Delphi study of the future of policing that this country faces possible riots and disturbances in the next several years that will make the riots of the 1960s pale in comparison. The reasons for these problems are many, but include changing demographics of our cities and other socio-economic pressures. He feels that one reason they haven't happened yet is because of the strong economy. This prediction, obviously, calls for being tactically prepared to meet these challenges. The paradox involves the pull of resources and job descriptions from opposite ends of the spectrum: being tactically prepared and interacting with the citizens. The tactical programs are attractive and high drama to both citizens and the police employees within the departments. However, Tafoya states those departments paying attention to the seemingly mundane daily tasks of working with many diverse community programs are those that are not going to have the serious riots and problems, while those departments concentrating on the "Us Versus Them" battlefield mentality that developed over the past years are very likely to experience them.

There are job tasks that are critically important to the job of policing that involve duties other than enforcing the law. Those involve the administrative functions of the department itself, as well as police and community relations and interacting with the community. As police administrators know, areas such as personnel, employee assistance, labor relations, planning and research, training, organizational development, and recruiting are also critical to the operations of any law enforcement organization. In many instances, the skills called upon to perform these functions may differ greatly from those called upon for the performance of the typical street policing function.

Many of us know officers who perform satisfactorily on the street, but don't set the world on fire. We have seen these same officers receive an assignment in other areas of the department and start performing like star quarterbacks. If the tasks of both assignments were analyzed, we would find that they were vastly different. Because the individuals in question had an opportunity to use their natural strengths, they performed very well. Being able to chart some of our strengths and possible weaknesses through understanding different personality types goes a long way in helping to understand why people sometimes don't seem to do well at some tasks and yet excel at others.

# 3  The Personality Types In Policing

People are usually attracted to occupations that appeal to their strongest preferences for doing things. As an example, have you ever wondered why accountants, as a group, seem to share some basic personality characteristics with each other, such as an attention to detail, established standards, seldom making errors of fact, and demonstrating a responsive structure and routine to what they do? Another example would be to observe those in the ministry, who have an inordinate concern, warmth, and compassion for others, along with an understanding of human nature. How about artists, who demonstrate a talent for creativity, inspiration, and sensitivity? If you observed the characteristics of people in many occupations you would see much similarity in personality characteristics and behavior in how they perform their jobs.

Compare the following police personality descriptions with the tasks of the job itself. Also compare the distribution of these preference types with the general population.

## Police Personalities at a Glance

### Sensing - Thinking

**Law Enforcement**  
70 percent

**General Population**  
32-42 percent

These are law enforcement professionals who prefer to take in and process information through their five senses and then make decisions through pure logic or objective reasoning. Some words to describe these officers are:

| | | |
|---|---|---|
| Concrete | Logical | Traditional |
| Decisive | Thorough | Observant |
| Practical | Impersonal | Sensible |
| Pragmatic | Factual | Structured |
| Direct | Analytical | Service Oriented |

These officers are generally extremely good at handling details and can absorb a great number of facts. They like being sequential, taking one step at a time. They enjoy working under a structured plan and like established ways of doing things, such as following a policy and procedure manual. They reach a conclusion through careful analysis and are generally patient with routine tasks. They are seldom wrong with the facts. They are practical and analytical. They are naturally brief and businesslike, and if forced to choose between tact and truthfulness, they will usually chose truthfulness. They may appear very serious, structured, and very literal to others.

They are not likely to be convinced by anything but reasoning based on solid facts. Appealing to their "feeling side" by using words such as "compassion, caring, sharing, gentleness, or sensitivity" will most likely fall short of the mark. They like to organize, control, and run things and usually have a natural, logical head for business. Because of their objective and realistic grasp of facts, they can usually do well in other occupations that deal with practical issues and analytical behavior such as banking, applied science, mechanical engineering, production activities, construction, doctors of surgery, and mathematics.

## Possible Pitfalls:

The activities of the law enforcement profession seem tailor made for STs. Using the basis of a structured policy or procedure manual to follow, they usually have the ability to handle rapidly unfolding, unpredictable chains of events while maintaining their "cool." They can wade right into an extremely complex and personally distressing situation exhibiting a very calm professional exterior. Because of this objective reasoning, however, they may fail to take personal issues of those individuals around them into consideration. They may appear to be blunt and insensitive and neglect basic courtesies that may seem unimportant or a waste of time to them at the time. They also may overlook long-range implications in favor of realistic day-to-day activities.

The STs seem to personify the "tough cop" image. They are what most people in and out of the profession picture when they describe how cops generally conduct themselves.

## Intuitive Thinking

**Law Enforcement**  
14 percent

**General Population**  
15-22 percent

These law enforcement personalities are the second most common in the profession. They are represented in police work and in the general population at about the same rate. They prefer to take in information through their "sixth sense" or Intuition and then decide, as STs do, through pure logic and objective reasoning. These officers can be described as:

| | | |
|---|---|---|
| Precise | Global | Goal-Oriented |
| Logical | Factual | Detached |
| Decisive | Strategic | Demanding |
| Conceptual | Visionary | Reserved |
| Cognitive | Theoretical | Independent |

They usually dislike detail and routine and may overlook the present while looking toward the future. They may forget specifics, but enjoy being involved in long-range, global activities. Since they take in information and process it through their intuition, they look for possibilities and usually do well with complex project activities. They enjoy challenges but may neglect routine tasks. Paperwork is not usually their long suit and they can become bored easily. They may appear "scattered and drifty" to STs because of this inattention to detail. They make decisions like the STs do, so they generally fit into the profession without feeling like an outsider. Because of this decision making preference, they also will tend to use truth over tact. They are the ones that are constantly coming up with new ideas on how to do things and may quickly move from one task to the next without finishing the preceding one. They communicate in global terms, often skipping steps and appearing to talk in circles. They reach conclusions rapidly and are challenged by complex problems. In addition to policing, they can do well in occupations that deal with research, law management, architecture, consulting, and education.

## Possible Pitfalls:

NTs can be naturally impatient with routine and may fail to focus on practical facts, issues, and details. They may need to concentrate and focus on one issue, making sure that detail is covered on that issue before moving on to the next. Because they prefer making decisions with pure logic, they can appear to be blunt and insensitive. They need to pay attention to people and their concerns. In this profession as in many others, NTs, because of their focus on global issues, tend to seek out job tasks that utilize this preference. Intuitive Thinking types are often found in supervisory or management positions, not necessarily because they like dealing with people, but because they like to manage complex tasks. In fact, dealing with people problems is not usually one of their favorite things. Because managing and leading people comes with the job of being an administrator, NTs often need to pay special attention to simple personnel issues such as thanking people for a job well done. In the realistic, impersonal, logical world of law enforcement, NTs can also personify the "tough cop" image.

## The Uncommon Feeling Types
## The SFs and NFs

### Sensing - Feeling

| Law Enforcement | General Population |
|---|---|
| 11 percent | 31-41 percent |

The officers that share this personality style are those that prefer to take in and process information through their five senses, as do the majority ST group, but prefer making decisions with a primary concern for people and the impact of their decisions on them. They comprise only 11 percent of the profession, far less than the percent that is represented in the general population. When compared to the 70 percent of Sensing Thinking types found in police work, we can see why the profession does not appear to be a caring, feeling, and compassionate one. Some characteristics of these officers are:

| Sociable   | Caring    | Considerate |
|------------|-----------|-------------|
| Practical  | Organized | Friendly    |
| Loyal      | Trusting  | Tactful     |
| Structured | Thorough  | Cooperative |
| Traditional| Observant | Concrete    |

These officers, as do the STs, seem to focus on detail and concrete reality and are practical, observant, and structured. However, since they make decisions through Feeling, they tend to be more aware of and sensitive to people and their feelings as necessary police work decisions are made. They seem to do very well in law enforcement tasks of community relations, media relations, personnel matters, and anything where people concerns or relations are paramount. They appear to be different from most other officers in law enforcement because of this people orientation. They are best with practical situations that need sound common sense and practical ability in dealing with people. In investigative matters, they are the ones that seem to be able to relate with the "crooks" best and usually seem to have an uncanny ability to cultivate strings of informants and sources on the street. Because of their preference for Sensing, they seem grounded in reality and are thorough and accurate. Being in the minority of police officers may cause some problems for them, especially with those with little seniority, as they may feel they don't quite fit in. In addition to doing well in law enforcement, SFs can do very well in health care, sales professions, teaching (especially K through 12), supervision, and community and religious service.

## Possible Pitfalls:

Because of their preferred decision making style that favors people and human values, they may not seem sufficiently "tough minded" to the rest of the officers. SFs themselves can notice this difference. It is natural for most people who belong to any professional group to try to fit in and act as the majority of those in the group act. As we know, law enforcement is generally a pragmatic, structured, impersonal, logical world and most in that profession behave in that manner. If SFs do not understand their own natural strengths and try to act as STs do, they may over-compensate by acting more blunt and insensitive than the STs themselves.

The SF officers bring a needed balancing dimension to the field of law enforcement, especially if they find themselves in tasks that involve continual relationships with people. In this new wave of citizen concern, they can be excellent community-oriented police officers.

### Intuitive - Feeling

| **Law Enforcement** | **General Population** |
|---|---|
| 5 percent | 15-21 percent |

This group of officers comprises only 5 percent of the law enforcement population compared to 15-21 percent of the general population. The NFs, along with the SFs, are what we refer to as the "uncommon types" in the profession. They prefer to process information through Intuition and then decide through Feeling, or social value. Some general descriptors of NFs are:

| Global | Gentle | Compassionate |
| Creative | Idealistic | Committed |
| Intense | Devoted | Empathetic |
| Perceptive | Friendly | Diplomatic |
| Conceptual | Congenial | Charismatic |

These officers tend to think globally and dislike routine and detail. They excel at long-range issues and conceptual projects and enjoy working with people. In this profession they also are the personnel-oriented individuals (e.g., chaplains, employee representatives, psychologists) and can be charismatic leaders. Most enjoy working in juvenile, community relations, and other community oriented jobs. They also can be excellent at research related activities where an insightful, long-range view is valuable. They are responsive to people's needs most of all, showing real concern for what others think and want, and they try to handle situations with due regard for others' feelings. They can usually lead a group discussion with ease and tact. Being conceptual in nature, they may try to take on too much, not paying attention to detail of projects they've already started.

Inasmuch as there are few of this type in the profession, they often stand out from the mainstream of officers as being different. This may cause some problems in adjustment, especially with a younger officer. The majority of these individuals who start in the profession drop out, feeling that the job was not as they expected it to be. When most NFs enter the field, they expect that the majority of the tasks will be to "help people and provide a service to community." When they find themselves in a profession dominated by structured, pragmatic, practical, logical, decisive, traditional, and impersonal appearing individuals, they leave. The same situation would occur if they found themselves in any other profession with the same characteristics, such as engineering, banking, mathematics, the military, and physical sciences. Those that stay in law enforcement bring a compassionate and global perspective to the profession. In addition to law enforcement, their strengths serve them well in behavioral sciences, art and music, religious service, psychology, and teaching, especially at the conceptual university level.

**Possible Pitfalls:**

As with SFs, NFs may not seem sufficiently "tough minded" to the majority of the ST officers. Additionally, as with SFs, NFs may find themselves over-compensating as they try to act as the majority of the Thinking types in the profession, becoming insensitive and autocratic, and appearing to lack all concern for people. This pull to operate in the Thinking function, which is not their preferred function and is therefore less developed, can be a source of internal and job-related stress. They, as do the SFs, make excellent people-oriented police representatives that can relate to the community well.

One way to demonstrate that people select jobs that appeal to their strengths of preference is to look at the distribution of cognitive styles across the U. S. population. According to 1996 estimates from the Center for Applications of Psychological Type reflects, approximately 32-42% of the population functions with the Sensing Thinking cognitive style; 15-22%, the Intuitive Thinking style; 31-41%, the Sensing Feeling style; and 15-21%, the Intuitive Feeling style.

Looking at police behavior and personality using the Jungian cognitive style framework began very recently. In 1978, Wayne Hanewicz, from Michigan State University, published research on law enforcement behavior using Jungian theory, to be followed during the 1980s by Ron Cacioppe and Philip Mock from Australia, Ron Lynch from North Carolina, Hobart M. Henson, Illinois State Police, and in 1991 by this author.

Several major studies that used the Myers-Briggs Type Indicator to confirm Jungian cognitive styles were consistent in their findings with regard to the percentages of types that were attracted to policing.

As you can see by looking at the distribution of personality styles across the law enforcement profession, a very small minority are NFs (those who prefer taking in information through Intuition and making decisions through Feeling). And yet, if you look at the research on other professions in the appendices, it is almost the reverse in some professions, particularly those involved in the helping professions.

The lack of NFs in the profession makes a lot of sense if a person were to look at the tasks involved in policing and law enforcement. The tasks are generally structured, finite, somewhat routine or repetitious, and based in present reality. The law is defined by what is or what is not a violation. Departments run on rules and regulations with policies and procedures for almost everything. The general description of the job of policing, as well as the function of a law enforcement agency within the community it serves, does not call for an overwhelming need for experimentation, variety, innovation, or creativity, but of stability, structure, and continuity. If you look at the descriptors or general characteristics or behaviors of various police officers, you will see that they seem to fit the description of the job well.

This is not to say that certain personality types should not be police officers, sheriff's deputies, conservation officers, state police, highway patrol officers, corrections officers, private security officers, or any other occupation involved in enforcing various laws, both civil and criminal. As you read on, you should easily see that all personality types can be and are very successful in any tasks they may choose to take on in this profession. Actually, those individuals that comprise personality types that are in the minority in the profession, such as the Feeling types, the NFs specifically, can and do bring refreshing depth and variety to the tasks of policing.

# 4    Differences in Communication

**A** real difference can be noted between the far greater number of Thinking types (STs and NTs) and the minority Feeling types (SFs and NFs) and the way each looks at and speaks of the tasks of policing. During conversations, the Feeling types talked about people constantly, using many colorful descriptions of street characters, and using the word "people" or "persons" many times. The NFs and the SFs often speak of their strong ability to communicate and relate to people on a personal level.

The use of the words people, folks, kindness, appreciation, and the like, are common in the conversations with Feeling types. The Thinking types, both NT and ST, describe things in more literal, general task terms. One ST deputy chief described his staff as "uniforms and clerks." Similarly, an NT captain described his transfers in terms of tasks rather than in terms of people. The STs typically discuss their jobs in the terms of performing tasks rather than the people they encounter while doing them, while NFs and SFs seem to describe their occupations in the context of dealing with violators and describing their associates as individuals.

## The NFs and SFs Dealing With People

The prime concern of Intuitive Feeling types while on duty is helping people. Their abilities are strongest in talking with and dealing with people. Note this comment from an NF deputy sheriff commander from a large metro sheriff's office:

> *My favorite calls were domestics. Back then there wasn't any domestic assault law so you just went in there and broke it up...it was kind of fun to go in and defuse the situation. I could talk to just about anybody about anything. I learned to like, and still like, an honest crook, a guy that makes his living being a crook. When you catch him he doesn't give you a lot of baffling bullshit...I mean periodically you run into somebody that there ain't any point to talking to, I then arrest his ass and throw him in jail. End of story.*

Another NF commander of a large agency speaks of his early experiences working in a rural area of southern Minnesota. The need for one to be able to talk his or her way out of a potentially dangerous situation in a friendly manner is a critical attribute:

> *Here in the city if you get into trouble you pick up the radio and you get help. My experience in the rural area was the best I ever had...it taught me so much that you have to talk to people. You learn that when a big Dutch farmer is drunk and he tells you he doesn't want to go to jail and to take him home and come pick him up Monday morning and we'll go to court, you can trust him and believe him. Here (in the city) you'd have more of a tendency to slam him up against the trunk and throw the cuffs on him. If you did that*

*down south at 2:00 a.m. you would probably go home by yourself with your handcuffs in pieces.*

Prior to this same individual being promoted and assigned to his present command, he was transferred to a precinct which had a reputation of the officers getting in fights with violators much more frequently than in the other precincts. He commented on why he felt that was happening:

*There's a reason the cops are being assaulted. Here the city's not that bad. We have some tough neighborhoods but any cop who is getting thumped a couple of times a week...there's a reason they are getting thumped...it's because of the way they may be treating people, in my mind. I just told them that it's no longer acceptable to treat people as less than human beings and if you do and you're wrong, I'm going to have your head. On the other hand, I'll stand right next to you if you do your job aggressively and right.*

He gave the officers several days of communication training on how to better interact with the public, and later commented that his complaint level was now down almost 40 percent, while the incidence of police injuries was down more than 80 percent.

One NF lieutenant, working for a rural sheriff's office, talked about first coming to the department:

*Yeah, I didn't even own a gun, I didn't have a uniform. I borrowed a friend's uniform...the sheriff gave me his gun and holster and said, just don't shoot anybody, just drive along. Don't make any traffic stops unless someone runs into you.*

He particularly liked the domestic calls in the rural areas. They tended to revolve around family problems such as the kid coming home drunk or the disputes between families:

> *They would say "Go take care of that guy" and I'd roll down there and was able to talk my way through that...I was very comfortable talking and dealing with those folks. I guess I didn't feel I was any better than the folks I was dealing with on the street...the citizens. I could easily see where I could be in the same position as they were. You have to find a way to deal with these folks on their level. I didn't write a lot of tickets because I didn't have to. I would walk right up to the kid and say I'm going to be here night after night, and if I see you doing that again I'm going to write you up. That seemed to work for me. I gained a lot of respect from the kids that way. I know there are other, more creative ways of dealing with something other than just a black and white hard-assed police attitude. I always thought people were individuals, and that every situation was different. So I look for the difference in people and treat them with what the situation needs.*

The police group representing the SF preference obviously shared many of the same social value and warmth considerations as the NF group.

> *For example, working in a poor neighborhood with a lot of minority group types, blacks and Indians, poor white people, a lot of welfare folks and stuff, I saw my job as really helping and serving and supporting these people. I would ride down the street and spend a lot of time waving at people as I went by and they would return the wave...or to stop at a playground and just*

> *talk to some kids in the field and stuff. I was more than willing to get involved in arrests and scuffles if it was necessary but the attitude of cops against the public and the public are the bad guys didn't wash with me. You can't treat people that way.*

The next comment also reflects the concern for people or people orientation, as spoken by a commander in a rural sheriff's department:

> *The sheriff that originally hired me made the comment that he didn't care if it was a little old lady that had a cat piss on her porch. He wanted her contacted because that was the most, the single most important thing in her life at that moment. I think the theory is very good. In law enforcement, it's the contacts, even though the mediocre calls aren't necessarily exciting...you take care of them, and I think you gotta keep that uppermost in your mind...what are the people problems, and to deal with them.*

To this deputy, the important part of the job involved treating people in an appropriate manner:

> *To me that's one of the biggest parts of the job. You gotta understand the citizen. You gotta have some feeling towards them and it can't always be negative. Just because they were going 70 in a 55 does not make them public enemy number one. I see the younger officers thinking that the speeders are bad, totally bad and I have a hard time handling that. I try to get it across to them that they are just citizens that we caught speeding. Maybe because of my nature I'm too far on the other end of the spread, but I'm trying...my goal is to reach a happy medium.*

Another example of general concern for people expressed by a Sensing Feeling type comes from an officer with twenty years seniority:

> *I went down and walked the beat near Douglas Avenue, which was our black neighborhood. I loved working down there. You had absolutely full latitude to do any kind of police work you wanted to and I liked the people and they liked me. It was a dream for a young policeman. There was all the police work in the world you could do. And fun type stuff. Old stuff like go to a crap game in the garage and run in and scream and watch them all go out the doors and windows and then you pick up the blanket with the money and dice on it and then walk down to the little old Black church and say to the administrator, here's a gift from the community for ya. Storybook stuff.*

> *I just liked the people. They were fun. They were energetic, they were also involved in a lot of crime, too. It was a police officer's dream. I just went down there looking at it as a real opportunity to have a lot of fun doing police work and that's just what it ended up being...it was every street character in the world, pimps, whores, junkies, anything you wanted was there, and in those days, the beat man had a tremendous rapport with these people.*

Another Sensing Feeling officer from the same department was a relatively large, quiet man who really enjoyed his assignment with the juvenile division. He was assigned to the group for several years and was then promoted to lieutenant. He supervised the unit for another year and was then moved to internal affairs. He said his favorite assignment was working juvenile. He really liked working with the kids and would have been content to stay there for the rest of his career. He felt that one had a better chance of making an impact on kids as opposed to working with adults. His time in juvenile was limited though, and he was assigned to internal affairs and then to family violence. The cases he handled there were sex crimes such as rapes, exposures, child abuse, and domestics. He took the transfer to get out of internal affairs because he didn't like the adversarial relationship with his fellow officers but he didn't like the family violence assignment at all:

> *It was a depressing place to work. Ya know, constantly handling child abuse cases and rapes and all that kind of stuff is hard work...emotionally hard. Ya know when you have to interview little kids about how they were molested by their father or what have you, it's not fun stuff for anybody. I would think my strongest point would be my concern for people. I don't know what term you would use, not necessarily a negotiator or counselor or anything like that, but I suppose when I was a detective I...had an ability to talk heated situations down as opposed to taking physical action right off the bat. Of course sometimes it didn't work and you had to take physical action.*

Another lieutenant, an SF from the same department, described his tour of duty in the jail of a major metropolitan department during the 1960s. His affinity for people is quite evident in the following excerpt:

> *No...it was horrible, it was like before the industrial revolution. It was a jail...a prison. We had people in there with communicable diseases...we had people in there that were so sick they were dying. I can remember the American Civil Liberties Union came over and forced (them) to come up and examine the jail. The poor guy never wrote a report...I think he went*

> *out of there so beat up because I told him...I have to work and live with these people every day. I take chances and give these people major medication to get them through because they are so sick. I give them alcohol, I give them anything to get them going because they are dying on me...I took the inspector back and they were like tiger cages. It was a jail built back in 1890. It had never been updated...it was a horrible year of my life.*

Much the same concern for working in and among people exists in the rural areas. One 6 foot 3 inch, 225 pound SF officer stationed in a rural sheriff's office began his career on the sheriff's water patrol. His uncle had been the chief of police in his home town and his father had been a police officer. This SF had been a religion major in college and is now an ordained deacon in his church.

> *I didn't care for the serious car accidents...(because of my) feeling for people. When they were hurt and so forth it bothered...I did find it bothered me...And that was something I had to learn...learn to overcome and live with. The contact with people, I would say for the most part, was good and enjoyable and that's what I enjoyed. Trying to work out and work with them or their various problems. I've had a hard time with some officers who seem to think that it's us against them and view most situations in a black and white manner. Most of the folks we deal with are honest folks and are just in a jam. They need a little consideration too.*

## STs and NTs and the Tasks of Policing

Sensing Thinkers (STs) and Intuitive Thinkers (NTs) are generally systematic and analytical, often to the point of being or seeming impersonal. As we contrast the descriptions of tasks and duties by SFs and NFs with those by STs and NTs (the majority of cognitive types in the law enforcement profession) you can easily see the difference in concern for people and concern for task.

An example of this orientation is clearly reflected by an NT captain of a major metropolitan agency. He commented on walking a beat. Note that he never mentions people in his description:

> *Walking...I kinda preferred that. I had the opportunity several times to ride what they called the district squad in a car and declined. Wanting to work there in the center of the action, so to speak. Something always going on, variety that we always like, and lots of learning in the center setting as opposed to way out in a district in the far end of the city where you just didn't have much exposure to policing activity.*

Contrast that description with the following colorful quote from an earlier comment by an SF officer in the same department.

> *I just liked the people (on the beat). They were fun. They were neat; they were energetic; they were also involved in a lot of crime. There was every street character in the world: pimps, whores, junkies...anything you wanted was there.*

In a discussion about what they liked about police work, one ST, who eventually became a deputy chief, stated *"I had a lot of freedom. I really enjoyed the variety. You just never knew what the next minute was going to bring. I enjoyed that."* He further commented on working traffic:

> *I almost have to say that I enjoyed sort of the cat and mouse game, trying to catch them doing something, that sort of became a competitive type thing. I really kind of enjoyed, strange as it sounds, taking care of crashes where you can really dig into things and you can...I even liked doing first aid and things after I got through it, ya know, I didn't particularly like picking up dead bodies and stuff like that, but I had a few rewarding experiences by saving a few lives along the way.*

Another ST enjoyed the traffic aspect of the job, although for him it was part of a larger fascination with the adventure of police duties. He worked with a state agency where the job was generally traffic-oriented, but, because they were sworn, licensed police officers, they could become involved in any law enforcement violation:

> *I liked the action, catching drunks...being on the patrol is a great job even if you don't like traffic. As a trooper, you've got the ability to roll on anything you want, I mean, you can help other police departments and when action's over you don't have to do any paperwork. You can go in on armed robberies, kidnappings, or chases, or just anything you hear, ya know, with a scanner. You know what's going on all over the metro area. And the other coppers are always happy to have ya show, ya know, they don't feel that you're stealing their thunder. So it was a good job...*

Another Sensing Thinking type, a deputy chief of a large metropolitan department, again commented on the excitement and variety:

*I started the job and found that it was extremely exciting...it was a huge challenge and the structure of the department was changing...I was offered three or four positions, I stayed in patrol only for a year or so and went to the former tactical squad (power shift) with the youngest charger on the department.*

He was transferred to a special research project which involved teaching civics classes in the school system. He taught criminal justice studies to ninth grade students. The aim was to try to overcome some of the racial tensions and to stimulate understanding of the criminal justice system. He was then promoted to sergeant and assigned to school liaison:

*I was out at Grant Junior High and Central High School which were inner city schools. It was a challenge. It was like transposing street crime into the schools and obviously had the stabbings and the shootings and the drug problems way back then...again it was very challenging and very exciting.*

As you can see from the comments, the focus of the STs and the NTs is generally on the excitement and variety of the job, without any real comments about the people. An ST lieutenant working for a state agency was a water patrol officer, drove an ambulance, worked for a sheriff's department as a desk officer, patrol officer, and jailer, and was hired as a narcotics investigator. He commented on narcotics investigations while working in the section:

*I loved it...the challenge, the role playing, the opportunity to...everything, every situation was different as far as I was concerned. You had to try a different approach or use a different line or use a different role...it was a target type situation or a goal out there*

> *you had to achieve. It was never dull. It was never boring. It will always be the highlight of my career...enjoyment wise.*

He moved from working undercover to organizing task forces and working complex drug cases. *"It was like putting a novel together, or pieces of a puzzle...it was really enjoyable."* He then transferred into the training area where he developed new courses for narcotics training.

As is the case with others sharing a Sensing Thinking preference, concern with task is evident in the above discussions of police work. In a long, minute discussion of the various transfers this ST officer was involved with, the only time people were mentioned was in the comment *"...you knew in your mind that the individual was a violator."*

This approach contrasts sharply with the comments by the SF chief of police in describing his task as *"...working in a poor neighborhood with a lot of minorities...I saw my job as really helping, serving and supporting these people and would ride down the street and spend a lot of time waving at people as I went by. I was always being accused by my partner of laying the groundwork for running for mayor."*

It's easy to identify differences in communication patterns between various personality types. The next chapter takes a look at how these various types of officers chose law enforcement as a profession.

# 5 Choosing Law Enforcement As A Profession

Most of us would assume we pick our occupations carefully. I mean, we are going to spend the majority of our lives in a profession so we must really concentrate on choosing the one that is best fitted for us, right? The truth of the matter is that in most cases, we usually seem to just "stumble" into an occupation which happens to suit us. However, if we look carefully back on our high school, early twenties, or early college years, we can see that we "tested" various jobs or tasks, quickly discarding or leaving those we didn't care for or weren't very good at. This "testing" was very subtle in nature, involving our study, our work, and our play. Eventually, for the most part, we found ourselves in an occupation which seemed to fit us. Most of us who found ourselves in law enforcement enjoyed it and were good at it.

Very few police executives could recall deliberately choosing law enforcement as the job they always wanted to have, however. The vast majority seemed to "just find themselves" there.

## The Intuitive Feeling Types Entering Law Enforcement

All but one of the NFs in this sample did not plan to become police officers. The one officer who planned to enter the occupation was really interested in becoming a game warden, but was too far down on the hiring list. He subsequently was hired by a rural sheriff's department.

*Basically, I wanted to help people. At that time I wanted to conquer the world and help people. My favorite course in rookie school was first aid...I knew it would help me in my job...helping people. When I responded to an accident I knew I would need to know the stuff.*

Other NFs in the sample came into law enforcement in various ways. One man entered law enforcement between his undergraduate and graduate work. He was playing music at a saloon and got to talking with the deputy that was serving as a bouncer.

*I was employed as a guitar player...studying sociology and psychology. I rode around with a deputy friend a bit and I liked it. I thought it was a pretty good deal. When I was sixteen I would pick up my girlfriend, put a buck's worth of gas in the Volkswagen and go drive down the back roads with the radio on. Now the county buys me a big fancy car with an AM-FM stereo radio with the red lights and sirens and all kinds of toys to play with and air conditioning and I go down the back roads listening to the tunes. I don't have my girlfriend with me but what the hell... they buy the gas.*

Another officer grew up in a lower middle class neighborhood where he liked and respected the police with whom he came in contact. That was in the days of beat cops on Lake Street and the park police, "...*and like I say, generally, they would be very helpful, nurturing, good people. Now if I would had met the bad ones, I might have felt differently...*" He met several probation officers because of the nature of the neighborhood and the fact that some of his friends were in trouble with the law.

> *So that's the way I came into it. I thought this is a good job, this is where you can make a difference in society. Kind of a uniformed social worker I guess is how I looked at it.*

Several other individuals, both now heads of their agencies, never wanted to get into law enforcement. One finished a double major in English and speech communications. Several of his good friends joined the police department as a way to get out of the draft. He had been urged to join as a way of getting out of going into the service, but really wasn't interested in the profession.

> *I wasn't going to be a cop. I didn't want to be a cop. So I got drafted. I did some AWOL apprehension while I was in the service...That was interesting and when I got out I thought a little bit about law enforcement, but I didn't want it for a career. I wanted to teach in college. My wife's father had been a cop and she told me she had no intention of being married to a cop...she said they drank too much...and always the half priced meals, the free coffee, 10 percent discount at stores, the whole image. So I looked around for a job and while at it, took the Fairfield City police test. They offered me a job...my wife was kind of upset about that, but I said, well it's different, it's a suburban department.*

The head of another large agency majored in business administration and earned a master's degree in Sociology. When asked why he became interested in the profession he replied:

*I wasn't. My dad was a cop, my uncles were cops, my cousins were cops and the last thing I wanted to be in the world was a cop. My aptitudes, as I was growing up, leaned more towards writing and history. I was a history major in college until it finally sunk in that if I wanted to make a living, I had better switch to something else. And still to this day, I don't know why I became a cop. I care a lot about people and I wanted to help people, I guess...*

## The Sensing Feeling Types Entering Law Enforcement

In the SF group, only two planned to become police officers. One stated *"Well, I determined in the sixth grade that I wanted to be a police officer and I never changed my mind through today."* The other said *"I guess I always was interested in police work from the time I was a teenager."*

The other six took the job because at the time it looked attractive.

*"Originally, I wanted to go in the seminary. Then I found out ya can't get married. Then I went from there to education...there wasn't a whole lot of opportunity in education without a high GPA, so I thought I should think about something else,"* said one. He spoke with a friend who was joining the St. Paul Police Department and decided to test for several other departments too. He applied for, and was accepted by, a major metropolitan police department. Another stated: *"I wasn't really looking for a career, I was just looking for an interesting job and the police department was hiring."*

An SF, who later became the chief of a large police agency, happened to be looking in the paper one day and saw an advertisement for police officers in the help wanted section. Before that, he had never had any desire to be a police officer but had always admired them.

As you can see, the vast majority of NFs and the SFs did not really plan to become police officers, as is the case with the NTs and the STs. As you go through the comments, continue to notice that the primary communication pattern of the NFs and SFs involves "people" and "helping people."

## The Intuitive Thinking Types Entering the Profession

As with the NFs and SFs (and STs as we will see in the next section), the choice of policing as a profession for NTs seemed to be more accidental than intentional.

An NT captain in a major metropolitan law enforcement agency, and a licensed attorney, became interested in law enforcement by chance. He enlisted in the army and picked jump school as a skill choice. He ended up in a military police group, was transferred to Germany, and assigned to a local criminal investigative division. He enjoyed the investigative work, and when he was discharged, he went home and took the police test. After joining the department, he was assigned to work midnights on the west side. *"I enjoyed the freedom. I always thought of police work as 'we were smarter than they were.' Sometimes it was a matter of trying to be smarter than they were and catch them."*

He went back to school, completed his degree, and then attended law school during the evenings. Shortly after graduating, he was assigned to research and development.

> *I liked the newness of it. I mean the projects we did. When you got an assignment, you had to create a way not only to get it approved, but to create a way to get it to work. The thing about research...as soon as you think you've got it all together, somebody else points*

> up another problem...and afterwards you just adjust and react and solve them. Some things were unsolvable, there was no solution to them...but a lot of people I work for, or work with, want simple answers to very complex problems and there aren't any, so that was frustrating.

Another officer, an NT director of a law enforcement agency, "felt a calling" during seventh or eighth grade to become a police officer. He attended college and became a community service officer for a suburban police department, and then became a licensed police officer for the same suburban department.

> (I worked) everything from traffic accidents to burglary calls, domestics, emergencies...I couldn't stand to process a crime scene. Just that detail work, the idea of getting there and looking for fingerprints...that was just worthless. But I did enjoy things like traffic...thoroughly enjoyed doing traffic...traffic accidents. I went into school. Medicals and domestics were fun.

Comments like that above were unusual. Most officers just seemed to fall into the occupation without a lot of forethought.

A third ring suburban chief of police, an NT, commented about becoming a police officer:

> "I was with the Vista project, that's Volunteers In Service to America. I was supervising the Vista project for the north and the south sides of Minneapolis. It was an interesting thing and I wanted to do something that was interesting with people." (This comment is unusual coming from an NT, but see his subsequent comment about social work.)

He became frustrated with the Vista project, dismissed some of his people, and made some public statements that the project was not serving people as it should. He later admitted, *"Well, I ultimately found out that social work in any form wasn't something I was interested in"* — a comment that is characteristic of an NT.

## Sensing Thinking and Law Enforcement as an Occupation

Interestingly, the STs, who are the vast majority in law enforcement, also seemed to "fall into" the occupation without a lot of conscious thought, as was often the case with the other types. One ST, who rose to a rank of deputy chief stated, *"Quite honestly, I was looking for a decent job."*

An ST command officer commented on her becoming a law enforcement officer:

> *I have always been attracted to policing. I have always wanted to get involved in the excitement...the fun stuff on the street. I had an uncle that was a cop and I used to listen to stories. I was always action oriented, even in high school. I love running a squad. It's the challenge of doing right.*

Most ST recruits, when asked why they wanted to become police officers, will comment without using the words "folks" or "people." They will comment about things such as the following:

> *I have always wanted to become a police officer. It is a good job, has great benefits, and it is highly respected. I have been in the Marine Corps up until now, in the signal corps, and now I want to give back to my community.*

Contrast that with recruits that prefer the Feeling function. They will typically say things such as:

> *I have been in sales and wanted to get into a profession that helps people. This is one where I feel I can make a difference in society and help people.*

Most of us would admit, even though we are in an occupation we really are satisfied with, the process of choosing that occupation appeared to be random. Again, what the vast majority of us do unconsciously is try numerous tasks, quickly discarding those we don't particularly enjoy doing or don't do well. There are some officers who may have felt somewhat uncomfortable in this profession but could do the job. They didn't particularly like it, but stuck it out and survived for a myriad of reasons including security, pensions, and other benefits. I would bet their preferred occupational strengths are probably in areas other than those strengths called for in the police profession.

# 6 Management Styles And How They May Differ

### The Intuitive Feeling Style in Management

The typical NF style of management is people-oriented and somewhat reflective in nature. An NF street sergeant in a suburban department characterized his management style as follows:

> *I think I've sacrificed maybe some short term performance for a long term relationship where in critical situations you may get performance that you may not have had otherwise. Some people think they should be a hard-nosed supervisor and I think they get begrudging results...if they stay behind somebody and crack the whip. This job relies so much on independent performance that (you don't want them to be) out in a car thinking what a jerk their supervisor is. They (the supervisor) can't be everybody's best friend, but if you take the abrasiveness out of it...you get better performance. That's just my style...that's reinforcing the idea of letting people do their jobs and valuing their input and valuing their talents...so I've been luckier than a lot of the other supervisors with what I consider to be high performance people.*

These interesting comments contain several elements that are very characteristic of NFs. The "sacrificing short term performance" principle reflects the conceptual, future orientation of the Intuitives. It also demonstrates a typical supporting attitude toward people.

Another aspect of this managerial style is the premise that administrative power ought not be abused. From this perspective, "they don't need a clock watcher, they don't need a baby sitter, and they don't need a slave driver." One NF sergeant really resented his previous supervisor who timed lunch breaks, coffee breaks, and was always hustling on the radio to see if he could catch someone doing something wrong.

> *It's January, it's 3:00 in the morning, 20 degrees below zero and you haven't seen a car on the road for two and one half hours. I don't care if you sit in a coffee shop for an hour because come July or August you aren't going to get a coffee break at all. And I believe that by the end of the year it's all going to wash out within five minutes, and I'm not going to lose sleep over five minutes and neither are you. And I would rather have you be open, and not try to be hiding things from me when you seriously have a problem. I want you to understand that I'm not being chicken shit and want you to understand that you can come to me first.*

An NF police chief of a suburban department described his personal management style as emphasizing the service nature of the police role. He stated that the best cops he has, and "ironically, the ones who also have the best enforcement record," are those who are the most service oriented.

> *Well, probably what I should do is send you a copy of our annual goals and you'll see where we are. We are primarily service oriented. Basically the idea is that my number one goal is that no one should ever have to call us twice. That means that if they call we will meet their needs. And I've taken it far enough that if it isn't in our jurisdiction we will connect them to the right one. We won't send people away saying we can't do that...because once they've reached us they have their link. I think I have a very open department. It's participatory in the sense that everyone has a chance to be heard and participate. I'm not democratic by any means, but if somebody has a good idea and if we adopt it, we let them run with the idea whether they are a patrol officer, sergeant, or whatever.*

Describing this same outlook differently, an NF captain in a large metropolitan agency commented, "I'm a people person, that's my strongest asset." In his opinion, he considers a potential decision's implications for the people concerned with the decision, before considering anything else.

"To make black and white decisions without considering the people involved, I can't do it, even though it would be easier if I could." This captain experienced a continual struggle with his superiors, whom he felt typified an autocratic management perspective. He was friendly with the people downtown (his superiors), but noted a distinct lack of people skills in the command. He merely hopes they will leave his precinct alone.

> *My people skills give me an extra dimension, but also it gives me more frustration because I'm dealing in a culture that historically does not consider the individual people involved... I've never been able to separate cold fact from the people involved. My philoso-*

> *phy is that we are all adults in an adult situation. You know the rules, you do the job. If you break the rules then I have to do something about it, but I'm not going to sit over you with my thumb. It seems to be working (management style)...I get the results that downtown is looking for. If I didn't get the results, though, I'm sure that management would think it's because I am more people oriented and in their eyes, not tough enough.*

One can see in the conversational style of the NFs interviewed that they used the word "people" often and seemed to be more oriented towards the individual. The same is true with SFs.

## The Sensing Feeling Cognitive Style in Management

The SF group represents their skills in dealing with people as their strongest managerial asset, as is the case with the NF group:

> *I feel that my approach is, let's find out what the problem is, approach that person, sit down with him or her and give them an opportunity to say what is or isn't. And that's where we (the feeling types) differ, because so many times my sergeants will go out and they'll blow off steam...it creates a real conflict in the department.*

Another chief (SF) of a major suburban metropolitan police department commented:

> *You have to be sensitive to people's needs. I believe in a chain of command, but it can shut good ideas down...there was a time when the boss came in and*

> *gave orders and the people did what they were told or lost their jobs...that's not a creative atmosphere in which to work...you need an environment where you can make good faith mistakes. If you go out and break the law or something, everything is gonna fall on you, but good faith mistakes you learn from and go on. We don't criticize and we don't punish for good faith mistakes. As an example, two officers stopped to pass on some information, maybe personal business, and when they pulled away, one cut a turn too quickly and wiped out the side of both squad cars. I wrote them a note and said I could see where I could do the same thing myself. They (the cars) are in the shop being repaired. Press on, don't worry about it. Because they didn't plan to do that, they will make sure for the rest of their natural lives they'll never do that again...why should anybody harp on the issue. It's not productive. Just put it behind you and get on. They feel more of a part of the organization...that the car is a piece of equipment and they as people are more important. You don't have to beat them up and say "Be sure and don't damage squad cars." They know.*

The emphasis on the people behind the job is evident in the comments of another SF chief of a large metropolitan police agency:

> *As far as a management philosophy, until somebody proves that they aren't to be trusted, I trust people. The thing is...the days of autocratic rule are gone...the idea that officers require extremely close supervision because they might do something wrong is childish. Unfortunately that does happen, but for the most part I think there should be an expectation that*

> *the people are dedicated enough...to go out and do it without being told...we all wear the same uniform, we've all got the same goals, we might have a different approach to these goals, but nevertheless we do have the same goals. My weakness is because I'm accessible, maybe too accessible to people (I've been told)...you're gonna get some hard lumps as a result of that. I think that because I try to be tolerant, I think I'm more than kind.*

Because of their Feeling preference and orientation toward people and their concerns, we might expect that SFs could get along well with other officers seeming to have the same orientation as they do. This was the case, especially when SFs recognized that associates who appeared to have the same work philosophy as they were also NFs or SFs according to Myers-Briggs cognitive styles.

> *In a lot of ways, we have some real differences of opinion too (speaking about an NF associate). But then again when he does something, in my own mind I know why he's doing it...I wanna give him a bad time about being too easy, even though I know I would probably do the same thing. (Speaking about a different SF manager and associate) Oh, I can understand, sometimes I don't agree, but I understand I might have made the same decision because I probably relate too well to where he's coming from.*

Similarly, an SF sergeant from a rural police department commented about his associations with a fellow officer sharing the same cognitive style.

> *John and I always have, ya know... John's on a different shift, but we've always been able to communi-*

*cate well together and I guess when there are certain department situations that come up, we always seem to look at them in the same way...we always seem to have the same perspective.*

## The Intuitive Thinking Cognitive Style in Management

NTs are usually referred to as being the standard executive type. Because the Thinking Judgment function is, by its very nature, a critical function, NTs are generally impersonal and objective, in addition to being matter-of-fact. They are interested in the broad picture and not necessarily in the details of the job. This appearance of impersonality is also true with the STs, who are the majority of the officers in law enforcement. Both of these styles share the same Judgment function, that of Thinking, making decisions with impersonal considerations rather than personal ones (Feeling).

When the decision-making functions of Thinking and Feeling are discussed in seminars, many NTs and STs make the comment "Hey, I have feelings too." Obviously, we all have and express feelings, but here we are not talking about the lack of having feelings, but the way we process information and speak about people and things. Usually, those who make decisions through the Thinking function lack the appearance of using the Feeling function as they comment and speak about things very analytically and pragmatically. As an example, read the following quote from an NT head of a large department.

*I don't like the paperwork. I delegate most of that to my lieutenant. Pretty much it's been pure delegation. One of the things I haven't done is I haven't had a formal staff meeting...I don't wanna waste my time or their time having a staff meeting to say "Hi, how are ya?" If something comes to my attention I'll fire it to one of my lieutenants or sergeants and say I expect you to take care of this...I delegate it out and expect it to be done, so I don't do a lot of follow up unless...it wasn't done.*

Another NT from a rural department with ten officers commented about the reason he likes his position:

*Autonomy. I like to be in charge. I like to be able to make a difference. I like to be able to see things that need a change and make that change. I need to keep the ideas going and the challenge is much more than coming here day after day.*

Note how the previous executive commented about change, which is the NT's strong suit because of the preference for variety, but never mentioned people or his desire to deal with them. Typically, as this illustrates, the NT command officer prefers to deal with tasks and make decisions with a very pragmatic logic and would prefer to leave the people issues to someone else.

## The Sensing Thinking Cognitive Style in Management

The STs, like the NTs, seem to describe their strengths in management as related to task management. They did, however, mention people more frequently in describing management style than when describing duties. This makes sense in that their primary job duties, at the time of the interviews, concerned dealing with people. Still, as demonstrated by the following deputy chief's description of his organization, STs tend to emphasize roles rather than the people filling them.

> *The people below me still have a direct connection to me and they are my ultimate employees or I'm the ultimate boss. We all...the four captains particularly all have interactions with the deputy chiefs...one controls the money and the transfers...another one has influence on investigations and discipline, and we run a rather open shop here so that they can interact with others.*

Another ST deputy chief, after a reorganization of duties, was relived that he didn't have to deal with a lot of people problems anymore. "I can do the others (people tasks)...but it's not much fun for me. Responsibility for a lot of other people's actions, ya know, that just wasn't much fun." He then went on to describe how he reorganized:

> *I was responsible for my own actions, didn't have a lot of subordinates to worry about. I put together a set of goals and objectives and I told the captains to write me a plan.*

You will notice with the words that this ST manager preferred to deal with tasks and not necessarily with people.

A Sensing Thinking deputy chief in charge of administration spoke about his managerial style as tough and forthright. Note his definite preference for dealing with task and not people.

> *Well, I never though of myself as being particularly tactful or diplomatic, but these are some of the things I would hear from my subordinates...he's fair, but hard, he doesn't take any crap and he can see through shallow excuses. You know, if I tell somebody to do it, goddamn it I expect it to be done. Period! I've gotten better at that too. The part I disliked most was dealing with the personnel issues...I have pretty good*

*organizational ability...in budget, planning and training.*

Suggesting that perhaps his present duties involved more use of "diplomacy than they were worth," this deputy chief remarked that he would go back out on the street "in a heartbeat" if his pay and benefits remained the same. He stated he often goes out on the street...he calls it "a little R and R." When he goes out to pull a shift, he said, "I go out to arrest drunks and throw 'em in jail. That's exactly what I do."

As the previous information and discussions indicate, the Feeling types, SFs and NFs, who comprise but twenty percent of law enforcement officers, are generally people-oriented, while the NTs and the STs, comprising over eighty percent of the forces, are task-oriented. This is one big reason why there are not a lot of "pats on the back for a job well done" in the profession.

The next chapter spends some time with the feeling types, which comprise, on the average, only twenty percent of the officers in the sworn ranks. Like everyone who finds themselves around people that are different, we all have a tendency to react in different ways. These officers, particularly the six percent who are Intuitive Feeling types, bring interesting additional dimensions to the organizations.

# 7 The Feeling Types And How They Differ

**Y**ou could assume that being a Feeling type in the Thinking world of law enforcement would be difficult and, in many cases, this is very true. Bearing in mind that Feeling types are in the minority in this occupation, one would expect they would feel a little out of place or different.

As I indicated before, several officers referred to themselves humorously as "oddballs." One Feeling type referred to himself as a "cigar store Indian standing in their (the department's) nice dining hall."

Despite their "oddness" relative to those with which they work, the NF managers all seem well adjusted. One reason for their lack of discomfort may be their relatively long tenure (18.9 years) and the ranks they hold. One would assume that many of the NFs who weren't comfortable left the police profession years ago feeling they didn't fit in.

A 6 foot 3 inch, 240 pound lieutenant with a rural sheriff's office commented that his size probably shielded him from potential aggravations and teasing from other officers:

> *Ya know, I never thought about it, but it probably has come to my aid more than I'm willing to recognize. They think "Well, he might talk soft but he*

> *looks like he's able to back it up." Even when me and a partner would go to domestics we'd separate the couple and then my partner would want to leave. I was the one that would want to spend a little extra time ya know...just sitting down and trying to reason with them...find out what the deal was and help them out a little bit. My partner would say, "Ah come on and let's get some coffee. We'll be back here again later tonight when they go at it again." If I wanted to spend a little extra time, I did, and I really didn't get any guff from my partner about being too soft and..come to think of it, not from any other cop either.*

Still, being a Feeling type could cause some personal pain being in law enforcement.

> *I would say, if anything, I was more caring, a lot more concerned. I think it caused me more emotional problems for myself because things would get to me. Pain bothered me more, I thought, than the average cop. I would let other people's pain bother me too much. I had an experience back when I was working patrol. I was on for three or four years. I had a double fatal chase. After that I almost quit. I always, I guess, from what other people said, had a lot more patience than other officers did. I could sit and listen more. In fact to this day even the dispatchers always say...one of them the other day said that I'm always even-keeled and very seldom can you see me get very excited and you seldom see me fly off the handle. I can remember one night some years ago we wrestled some guy out of his house during a domestic...took him to the hospital for his drinking. He wasn't very happy. I went by the hospital to see him*

> *several days later. He couldn't believe that I would do that...and he wasn't somebody I knew either.*

Another NF deputy sheriff shift supervisor knew he was different from the usual police officer.

> *Being different didn't bother me as much as it seemed to bother other people. So they must be the ones that have a problem with where I stand. I don't have any particular problem with where they stand, I don't wanna stand there, but I'm not going to deny them the right to stand there...so when the new hires come on and ask what the hell's this guy all about, they say, don't worry about him, he isn't gonna bother ya...hey, we have this cigar store Indian in our nice dining hall, but other than that, we still have a nice dining hall, he's a nice Indian, but he's still here.*

This same officer, who holds an M.A. degree in Psychology, commented that the demographics of the department were changing. It used to be that in order to be hired, an officer had to be from the local area. Additionally, in the early days, military veterans were given preference in getting jobs in civil service. Now, however, that is not necessarily the case. The department is now made up of individuals from all over the state and has grown to over 125 people. Many new officers coming on now don't have a military background. This supervisor feels that as the pool of more experienced employees grows larger, his deviation from "true north" becomes less noticeable. He believes that the more diverse a police officer's background, the more accepting officers are with them being different than they are.

Another NF captain really enjoyed working the road (accidents and all), but he did not enjoy arresting people.

> *I did learn early in my career that I didn't like to arrest people. I always enjoyed driving fast...it makes the blood run, but I always felt bad in the routine traffic arrests. I wish I could give all those people a warning. The whole time I worked the road I never got over the fact I didn't like arresting people. I've worked the metro, specialized in training, taught defensive tactics, first aid, night stick use, from range officers to whatever...and I still don't like arresting people.*

Another Intuitive Feeling captain, who stands 6 foot 2 inches tall (230 pounds), commented about his differences from most other police officers:

> *Yes, I was different and it bothered me if somebody made a comment about "how the hell can you be in this job being so soft. I would have punched that guy long before that." (I was talking and negotiating with a violator long after they would have taken some physical action.) Or they would be surprised if I got into a scuffle with someone because they felt that I usually would rather talk than fight. I've been in a shooting incident which came out okay. I ended up lifting weights with the guy who was later convicted of murder. I'm sure that didn't endear me to other officers in my station.*

An NF street sergeant with a large suburban law enforcement agency spoke about his different approach to dealing with problems:

> *A lot of times I would come to the same conclusion as to what course of action to take in a given situation, but I think I took greater pains to smooth a situation*

> *over a little bit. When you had to tell a citizen or somebody that they were under arrest...I tried to not make it a personal thing between myself and a suspect or something...like some officers feel that the suspect offended them personally so they are going to jail. I have always had a fairly aggressive enforcement stance...I don't apologize for people going to jail or arresting someone, but I have always made a strong effort to keep people satisfied. I want them to know that I'm not judging them personally, but judging what they have done and that's why they are in the position they are in. I've probably spent more time, maybe more time than I should have sometimes, hanging around to talk to people and tell them what we did or didn't do.*

SFs recognize they are somewhat different than most of the other police officers in the way they deal with people. As an example, this Sensing Feeling officer stated:

> *I tended to pick partners that were similar to myself. Ya know oftentimes we handled, ya know, we always worked as a pair, and I wouldn't have picked a partner that would go blasting right in a place and start punching people out, I mean that is not my style.*

Interestingly, he said he felt he was the exception when he first started police work twenty years ago (late 1960s), but felt that he would not necessarily be the exception now. He felt the concern for people and basic rights and dignity was more important than it was many years ago.

> *I think law enforcement is changing. I think the make-up of the police department was quite different.*

*More females, more diversified work force...higher education level...*

Recall that the NF sheriff's deputy who called himself a "cigar store Indian" said the same thing regarding the changing make-up of the police department.

The deputy chief (SF) of a large metropolitan agency commented that he was highly enforcement-oriented with "... the highest misdemeanor arrest rating in the station for the four years I was on a power shift." He characterizes himself as "highly enforcement oriented, but by the same token, wanted to deal with satisfied customers."

> *You can arrest the husband and father for domestic abuse or whatever it happens to be, but you are still dealing with the wife and you're still dealing with the kids and you are leaving the image of the department there. And I was always sensitive to that...I worked with some older guys that didn't necessarily have a high regard for enforcement...carried candy and stuff to give to kids on domestics and I was always touched by that kind of involvement. You are serving those folks and you've got to be selling yourself...always.*

Another Sensing Feeling captain from a large metro agency characterized himself as being different from the other officers in his department. At rookie school he was quiet and reserved. "I didn't fit into the military academy thing at all. I had to get out on my own. I didn't like that regimentation." When asked if he felt others perceived him as being "soft" he said: "No, not all of the time. I can be pretty miserable if I have to be. I don't like to, but I can. I used to have a real quick temper."

A Sensing Feeling sergeant, stationed in a rural sheriff's office, commented that he didn't think much about being different from other officers for the first part of his career because he worked alone most of the time. When he thought about the question he commented: "Ah...with probably the majority of law enforcement officers, I've been told that I carry my feelings out on my sleeve too much."

A rather outspoken SF lieutenant from a large metropolitan agency characterized "feeling differently" than most other officers thusly: "I'm much more friendly with people than most cops. I enjoy people. I like dealing with people. I like talking with people."

## What Happens With Most of Those Who Feel "Different"

An interesting situation surfaces here. If someone comes into the police profession, or any profession for that matter, and finds they feel "out of place," they would most likely have a tendency to leave and find some other employment where they felt more comfortable.

Several colleagues and I conducted a study at a technical college in Minnesota with individuals who were part of a police training class. In Minnesota, if you want to become a law enforcement officer, you must first attend a two year program at a technical college, university, or community college and then take a "skills course" for an eight week period of time. This then enables you to be licensed. The new students in the law enforcement class were given the Myers-Briggs Type Indicator along with a series of other assessment instruments and tests. The distribution of the cognitive Judgment styles of this class was 80% Thinking and 20% Feeling, the same general Myers-Briggs distribution for a group of veteran police officers with twenty years on the job.

The results of this distribution would lead one to believe that **rookie cops do not necessarily become socialized into being less compassionate cops after being on the job for a period of time.**

It would appear the occupation's tasks attract those whose strengths are matter-of-fact, practical, logical, direct and rational, fair, structured and just, in a logical sort of way. **This would seem to explain why cops, who generally appear to be cold, condescending, serious acting, and authoritarian could appear to be that way as a result of preferences which Jung felt were present at birth or shortly thereafter.** This is generally contrary to some sociologists' theories of the 1960s and 1970s that police working personalities were the direct result of the influence of veteran cops on rookie cops. Many sociologists felt that if law enforcement agencies specifically recruited warm, feeling, and compassionate individuals, the police services would become more warm and compassionate. The above results seem to indicate that warm, nurturing, compassionate individuals would not necessarily be attracted to the profession anyway, due to the nature of the tasks required in performing in the profession.

It was interesting to note that one-half of the Feeling types in those law enforcement classes left before their two year graduation. Most of them cited "incompatibility" with the program. This would seem to reinforce the issue that people are attracted to jobs in which they can use their strengths. As a cross check, we administered the instrument to two more successive classes, and in the next several years the distribution remained the same as that of veteran police forces.

## Physical Size May Affect Success for Feeling Types

This brings up additional interesting issues. All but one of the Intuitive Feeling types interviewed was at least 6 feet tall and all weighed at least 200 pounds. The one exception was 5 foot 10 and one-half inches, lifted weights and was noticeably muscular. The law enforcement profession is primarily masculine, characterized by the rough and tumble, physical situations that the media portrays. Fighting, chases, shootings, struggles, and macho images are portrayed continually. I would bet that, because of the large, imposing physical size of these officers, their "deviation from true north" by displaying compassion was not challenged as it might have been had they been smaller in stature.

For example, if a police officer were a smaller male with a Feeling decision preference, he may be intimidated by other officers through kidding, cajoling, or teasing. As these Feeling type officers began to realize that they were different from the vast majority of other police officers, they may decide that law enforcement wasn't for them. I do not believe this to be necessarily true in the case of women police officers who are typically smaller in stature than their male counterparts. In fact, precisely because they are women, male officers might expect compassion as a cultural norm for them and not subject them to extensive teasing as they would male officers. Being a Feeling type in law enforcement may be a self-fulfilling prophesy as far as job tenure is concerned. Many Feeling types may tend to be uncomfortable and may leave for another occupation, which means there are more Thinking types represented. But the critical issue is, as you can see from the interviews, those few remaining Feeling types who desire to remain for whatever reason give the occupation an interesting depth.

The reverse is probably true for the helping professions, such as social workers and probation personnel. In those professions the majority of decisions are made through social value and the majority of the people in these occupations are Feeling types. A person with an impersonal, basic, practical, matter-of-fact, Thinking function may feel uncomfortable with a group of people that are continually expressing compassion, human concern, and are gentle, sensitive, and caring. Both, naturally, want to associate with groups of individuals more like themselves.

We need to recognize that the tasks involved in the policing profession are those that appeal to the Thinking types. Many of those tasks are structured, sometimes cold, generally impersonal, logical, objective, and matter-of-fact. Sociologists' desire to have warm, nurturing, caring, feeling police agencies that demonstrate a lot of compassion may be impossible to a large extent. We may, and really should, teach officers to be more people-oriented. Because of the nature of many of the job tasks in policing and their attraction to the Thinking types, most individuals in the profession will probably not be people oriented naturally.

# 8   Women in Law Enforcement

As we know, women have been a part of the law enforcement profession for many years. It has been just within the past twenty years or so, though, that they have really been allowed to function as full fledged police officers on the street doing the same tasks as the male officers have been doing. Prior to being assigned to working the street, they were assigned to areas that administrators stereotypically felt they would do best in, such as in the records sections, juvenile bureau, or sex crimes. Many women were not allowed to wear uniform trousers, but had to wear skirts and hose in 100 degree plus days. They were allowed to carry weapons but only in their purses, not in a holster on their hip. Early on, the conventional wisdom was that policing was a man's profession, that women tended to be physically weaker than men, and that the job on the street was probably too tough for women. People felt that since women were naturally compassionate, they could best use their inborn compassion on sex and juvenile cases.

It is true that many females generally tend to be weaker physically than men in upper body strength. Because of this, women may not resort to physical force as often as male officers do, which can be reflected in numerous studies stating that female officers have fewer brutality complaints than men have. Few calls, however, require the use of brute force and there are usually several cars as backups at any scene. Additionally, various self-defense skills used by both men and women can make up for lack of upper body strength.

Some sociologists have felt that an increase in female police officers on a force may increase police "sensitivity" toward citizens, comments that some women police officers disagree with as they don't want to be seen as "weaker" than men. It is generally true, however, and many studies indicate, that women do possess better communication skills than men on the whole, and that some women can use this ability as an alternative to the use of brute force.

Women have been a part of the mainstream patrol and administrative duties of various law enforcement agencies for many years now, and it is quite evident, and has been so for a long time, that female police officers do as well on the street as males can.

A colleague and I had an opportunity to present a seminar on police personalities and to administer the Myers-Briggs Type Indicator to 82 female police officers who were among a group of over 500 women attending the International Association of Women Police conference in St. Paul, Minnesota, in 1990. The seminar took place on a Thursday, four days into the conference.

Prior to taking the instrument, the women police officers were cautioned several times to be sure to try and answer the questions as they truly felt they *personally* preferred, not as they felt their occupation or specific organizations expected them to be.

**Table 1: Women Police Officers at the International Association of Women Police Conference**
**N = 82**

| Cognitive Style | | Percent | Number |
|---|---|---|---|
| Intuitive-Feeling | NF | 20.80 | 17 |
| Sensing-Feeling | SF | 24.40 | 20 |
| Intuitive-Thinking | NT | 17.00 | 14 |
| Sensing-Thinking | ST | 37.80 | 31 |
| Totals | | 100.00 | 82 |

It is interesting to note that the frequency of the Intuitive Feeling cognitive style in this group of female police officers resembles what you would expect to find in the general population. The frequencies of the Sensing Feeling and the Intuitive Feeling cognitive styles also resemble the general population, but the Sensing Thinking percentage is higher. The SF and ST preferences being the highest in these 82 women makes sense in that the occupation calls for Sensing strengths. The 45.2 percent preferring the Feeling function in making decisions is vastly different than that of other police officer samples comprised primarily of men.

The police occupation generally reflects the Sensing Thinking preference with the Intuitive Feeling preference being greatly under-represented, but here we have a group of female police officers who tend to resemble the general population.

Nationally, women police on the whole comprise approximately nine percent of the total number of officers in various departments. In some departments in my study, there was only one single female in the sworn ranks. In spite of women being under-represented in police forces on the whole, the interesting fact is that the female's type preferences in this study reflected the general population and not that of a typical group of male police officers.

Taking into consideration that the vast majority of male police officers are Sensing Thinking or Intuitive Thinking, females in the police profession may tend to reflect those behaviors they feel are expected and valued in the profession rather than their "true" type. In many studies, women have mentioned that they have really tried to act like the men in an attempt to fit in at the predominantly male agencies. Most have found, however, that modifying their behavior into what they think is expected doesn't really work in the long run.

In the case of police tasks and general attitude, compassion and social value is not necessarily appreciated, nor expected in the occupation. Any possible confusion in cultural attitudes and how a person feels they need to behave to be accepted is most likely to take place in the Thinking-Feeling area. Culturally, people often equate feeling, compassion, and warmth with feminine attributes, and cold, hard logic and rationality with masculinity. It is clearly apparent that both men and women can perform the cold, hard tasks of policing equally as well, although perhaps through a different methodology.

The results of the instrument the women took while attending the conference raises some very interesting questions. Being away from a work setting in a casual, relaxed conference setting may have produced more valid statements of how a woman really sees her personality style, particularly after being coached several times to answer questions in a personal way rather than an occupational way. Additionally, being in a supportive group of over five hundred female police officers over five days, and perhaps feeling more validated through sharing law enforcement experiences common only to women, may possibly have contributed to a more realistic picture of how women police actually are. As stated before, being in a predominantly male occupation really involves intensive peer pressure to "conform to the majority" in many instances of police work. Being in a group of female police at a conference may have reduced the result of peer pressure to act as the majority of male officers would act back in their own departments.

Another consideration is the dynamics of why women in policing would want to have a police conference specific to their gender. Obviously, there are issues confronting females in law enforcement that are vastly different from those confronting male police officers.

There are several interesting issues to consider.

- In Minnesota, of the students entering higher educational institutions for the expressed intent of becoming a police officer, twenty-five percent are women. Of those graduating, only five percent are women. Women may see entering the law enforcement profession one way as they begin school and then see it in a much different light part way through, and, as a result, leave.

- Women may tend to bring more personal value and compassion to the field, but, when surrounded by a majority of Sensing Thinking types in the educational process, and perhaps feeling they may approach problems differently, decide the occupation is not for them.

A thought for the future may be, if the nature of the job of policing changes, would it appeal to more SFs and NFs, thereby attracting more to the occupation? Would the occupation then begin to change because of more concern for human value? Would it continue to attract and retain more Feeling types because their comfort level would be growing as the majority of STs and NTs diminishes? Would this occupation resemble the general population, as far as Jungian typology and Myers-Briggs cognitive styles are concerned, if more women were to become a part of the occupation and stay?

**During our presentation to this group at the National Association of Women Police conference, we asked them what personality and behavior attributes, in their opinion, were important for being a police officer. First on their list was the ability to communicate; second was the ability to make a quick, sound decision; and the third was the need for compassion.**

These are interesting thoughts, particularly in this time of public complaint about the apparent lack of compassion in the field.

# 9    Possible Weaknesses Of Each Style

All of the different styles bring certain strengths to the profession. Obviously along with those strengths people would also display some of the weaknesses or pitfalls of those various styles.

An understanding of police personality according to Jungian cognitive styles brings us new insights into how people perform on the job and the effect that possible weaknesses in taking in information and making decisions can have on their performance. Usually, when people become aware of their strengths and weaknesses and how both affect their performance on the job, they begin to work to deal with both better.

## Potential Weaknesses of Intuitive Feeling Types

Despite strengths, Intuitive Feeling types speak of weaknesses that make them seem different from Sensing Thinking types. Some of the potential areas in need of development by those preferring the NF functions are:

- They may not be seen as sufficiently tough-minded to Sensing and Intuitive Thinkers;

- They may try to please too many people at the same time or appear "drifty" or scattered;
- They may need to pay more attention to the details of the task and to the concerns of people.

As one example, an NF chief of a large agency recognized his being different from others as being politically vulnerable. He had been told by others that he was too humane. "You're going to get hurt. You're letting your feelings interfere with your operation," was how they put it.

Another Intuitive Feeling type, a chief of a large metropolitan agency, was aware of police personality and the MBTI. He purposefully appointed an individual that he knew was good at detail (an ST) to "handle the details." He spoke of conceptualizing what needed to be done and then asking his assistant to fill in the blanks and make it work. He knew his strengths were not in handling the details and that he would not do as good a job as the ST. As a result of their teaming together and using both strengths, the tasks were handled well.

Two of the individuals in the NF group had difficulties switching from the street to management because of their concern for the feelings and friendship of others. Simply put, their concern for people got in the way of their managerial roles.

One NF characterized it as follows:

> *When I became a supervisor, I guess I didn't know how to handle that. I felt that staying in that character of being one of the guys didn't work out because a lot of the guys didn't respect that, they didn't work for me, they didn't do their job, they thought that what the hell, this guy is...well you know, so I came on a bit too strong and too severe and that wasn't supported by the department so I've been spending the*

*last few years backing way off and trying to be more understanding...I tend now to be a little too nice.*

He commented that he feels more comfortable now in being a "bit more friendly, and warmer. Sometimes you lose who the hell you are in trying to be someone that you are not."

As expressed in the above comment, some Feeling types may have a tendency to become "hard-assed" as supervisors. This can be explained by looking at type dynamics as follows:

An NF personality type would have Intuition or Feeling as dominant and auxiliary functions, with Thinking and Sensing as tertiary or inferior functions. Individuals often have difficulty being someone that they are not. According to type dynamics, individuals in an organization whose tasks are primarily Sensing and Thinking, such as law enforcement, but whose strong preferences are social value (Feeling), may try to emulate ST traits and overcompensate resulting in a more strict personal interpretation of behavior. They may become very autocratic and hard in an attempt to act as those around them, and deny their feelings and concerns for people as inappropriate for those in the police occupation.

On two occasions, when I explained Jungian personality theory to police managers, tears formed in the eyes of two individuals who showed NF preferences. Both had characterized themselves as real "hatchet men" at work. They said they had pushed their concern for people aside, believing that concern didn't belong in management, particularly in management of a paramilitary organization such as a law enforcement agency.

Personality theory assumes that people are born with a predisposition to prefer performing some functions over others. For example, a person who naturally has developed Sensing in a highly specialized way is likely to be an astute observer of the immediate environment. While attention is directed to the specifics of the environment, this person may spend less time using the opposite function, in this case, Intuition. When a person enters a profession, understanding the tasks and activities needed to successfully perform in that profession are extremely important. Tasks and activities can foster development of preferences or force the use of preferences that are weaker. When we are not using our natural strengths, the profession or tasks may seem to be less satisfying. As we know, the law enforcement profession attracts primarily those with a Thinking preference. It seems clear that some individuals in law enforcement who prefer the Feeling function may overcompensate while trying to balance the use of pure logic (Thinking) with social value (Feeling) and become dictatorial and autocratic.

Indeed, this personality dilemma seems tailor-made for an occupation like law enforcement. Generally speaking, law enforcement attracts primarily STs. This being the case, when NFs become cops, they either have to try to fit in by "copying" others and their actions, or just accept their differences and try to adjust. Many cannot adjust so they leave, stating they "just didn't fit in." Others, when they try to act in areas which are not their strengths, may become frustrated and feel they are not being "true to themselves."

It is hard to act like someone you aren't. You can pretend for a while, but it takes a lot of effort and usually results in neurosis and/or generalized exhaustion over a long period of time.

I should note that the potential problems of being with those that don't act like you do goes both ways. If a Sensing Thinking individual were to find himself or herself "trapped" in a warm, nurturing, unstructured environment, such as that created by a Intuitive Feeling supervisor, he or she might be extremely uncomfortable. This type of environment would typically be characterized by lots of smiling, chatting, hugs and pats on the back, and lots of overt concern for the employee's welfare. For the STs a structured, realistic, practical, systematic, and concrete task-oriented organization would be much more preferable because of its consistent and systematic rules.

An excellent example of imbalance, or "trying to act in a different way than is natural," was noted in the comments of an Intuitive Feeling commander assigned to a southern precinct. He had a reputation of being strict, "too strict by today's standards." To him it was "my way or no way."

*To tell you, I damn near quit in the first two or three months. I decided this stuff wasn't for me (supervision). I felt like a fish out of water. I felt uncomfortable supervising guys that had three times the time I had on the force. I had some times that I went nose to nose with some guys and I hadn't backed down and I stumbled a few times. I had my boss tell me to lighten up a little bit. Some of the guys perceived me as maybe a pushover. I took a survey a couple times a year on how I was doing...one thing that used to come up pretty frequently was the hard line I took on (my) people.*

This commander acknowledged that being a supervisor has been hard on him. As a result, even though he had chances for several additional promotions, he turned them all down. He is looking forward to retiring and doing something other than law enforcement.

## Potential Weaknesses of Sensing Feeling Types

Even though these officers make decisions based on Feeling, SFs possess a strong reliance on Sensing, which is why they fit into the profession as well as they do. The Sensing grounds them in concrete issues and interactions. There are, however, several pitfalls for SFs and some of these resemble the issues the Intuitive Feeling types have to deal with:

- They may not be seen as being sufficiently tough-minded (the same problem as NFs);

- They may need to consider global issues as well as present considerations;

- They may attempt to avoid conflict because of their feeling for people.

As I mentioned before, one SF commented about being too soft, and recognized this characteristic as making him politically vulnerable. The other police manager had said, "You're too humane, you're gonna get hurt. You are letting your feelings interfere with your operation."

There appears to be a pronounced job focus among the SFs, as is usually the case with the mainstream STs. They typically do not report many outside interests other than those around law enforcement. Even within the field itself, they exhibit fewer dramatic role changes than others, particularly the NTs. Apparently the SFs seek to do their jobs well, but may not necessarily look for lateral or upward transfers. They, for the most part, seem to be tied up in performing their jobs in an excellent manner.

## Potential Weaknesses of the STs — the "True Norths"

The activities of a beat cop seem perfectly suited to the inclinations of an ST. They feature rapid, unpredictable chains of events in which maintaining one's "cool" is essential. However, there are some possible weaknesses that may affect some individuals preferring the Sensing Thinking functions also:

- They may neglect important personal issues as they concentrate on pure objectivity;

- They may overlook long-range implications for day-to-day activities as they usually enjoy and tolerate routine well;

- They may appear blunt and insensitive to those that they work with and to members of the community.

Of the group of ST managers interviewed, several commented on the fact that they didn't like to deal with personnel problems. One was relieved when a personnel function was re-assigned from him to someone else. None felt they were different from the majority of other police officers, and some even pointedly asked if they should feel differently from other police officers.

Based on this information, it seems clear that STs like and feel comfortable within the police culture's emphasis on impersonal, logical interaction. They seem to sense they fit in and may even yearn for the opportunity to return to this style of behavior if placed in other positions which require a more personal, warm and human approach.

In contrast to the NF who described himself as a "deviation from true north," the STs, who personify the "tough cop," are what most people, in and out of the profession, refer to as the "true north" barometers of how cops usually conduct themselves.

## Potential Weaknesses of Intuitive Thinking Types

Like their ST counterparts, the NTs also personify the "tough cop" and are referred to as "true norths" in the profession. Their preference for the Intuitive function gives them a facility for insight, rapidly making connections, and seeing long-range implications of their actions and of police policies.

Some of the potential pitfalls for those preferring the NT function might be:

- An NT may be too impersonal and unappreciative of input from others;

- They may become forgetful of current realities;

- They could find it hard to focus on practical details and have a problem carrying issues through to the end.

Interestingly, none of the NTs commented on being too tough or not appreciating people enough. This makes sense as they make decisions with pure logic, as the STs do, and generally would not even think that they may not appreciate people. While many NTs in law enforcement act impersonally, they may not believe that they do. Most of us do not have the insight to see whether we do or not. This seems particularly likely in the context of our work in the realistic, impersonal, and logical world of law enforcement.

As far as lack of attention to detail is concerned, one NT stated that he was never any good at remembering names, license plates, or details of a homicide. Another commented about his partner "driving him crazy with constant detail."

Another example of inattention to detail concerned an incident with an NT manager of a police academy who called a meeting with five ST subordinates for twelve o'clock noon to discuss various instructional issues. As the meeting progressed, the STs became irritated at the length of the meeting. The NT manager explained that he had told them the length of the meeting in the memo he had sent them. The STs protested that he had not, nor had he mentioned that they should cancel their other classes, nor where the meeting was to be held. The NT supervisor retrieved the memorandum he had sent, and after re-reading it, realized that he had neglected to mention not only the expected length of the meeting, but also the subject matter and where the meeting was to be held. He later mentioned that he had apparently "just assumed" he had furnished all of the details to the others.

# 10  Police Conflicts With Other Professions

Among cops, "newsies," social workers, and "shrinks" there has been a long history of misunderstandings and conflicts in communication and methodology in how each does their job. Police ask that details be withheld from a story and then see them in print; on other occasions newspaper accounts lack the details that police think are necessary to tell the full story. Ask any group of police officers to put up their hands if they have worked on a case or an incident and read about it the next day in the paper. Then ask them if they hardly recognized the story as their case and the hands stay up. This is certainly not the case with every reporter who ever came around a police precinct, or with every social worker who dealt with juvenile divisions, but generally there has been misunderstanding and conflicts with those professions more than others. Social workers and case workers in corrections often feel that police lack compassion. They hear the side of the story from the arrestee and allege mistreatment or lack of consideration. Victims Rights activists are often critical of the impersonal style of many police officers during domestic violence cases. Here a woman is in crisis, may be acting rather emotionally and hysterically after months or years of abuse that have led up to this situation, and "in walks a male in uniform with an attitude."

Describing each other in less than glowing terms from "jack booted Nazi cops" to "bleeding heart liberals," these professions look at each other in somewhat less than understanding ways. We may not have considered that the objectives of each job were different for each occupation. A person would think, though, that even if the jobs were different, they all deal with the field of criminal justice. So what could be the difference that makes people in these occupations look at issues in a way different than law enforcement?

A look at these various occupations through Myers-Briggs cognitive styles reflects some interesting reasons which can help explain why these inherent differences exist. We already know that the predominant cognitive style in the police profession is Sensing Thinking (ST), while the least represented style is Intuitive Feeling (NF). An interesting fact to note is that the CAPT data bank reflects a sample of editors and reporters, along with a sample of social workers, as having predominant cognitive styles of Intuitive Feeling (NF), which is the least represented in law enforcement. No wonder both occupations look at things differently.

The majority (42 percent) of this sample of editors and reporters shows a preference for Intuitive Feeling, while in the police sample, the Intuitive Feeling types were only 6.3 percent. With this vast difference in the way these people would look at issues, no wonder there is somewhat of a rub in relationships and a lack of understanding between the two professions.

## Editors and Reporters:

> **Table 2: Editors and Reporters**
> **N = 113**
>
> |  |  | Percent | Number |
> |---|---|---|---|
> | Intuitive-Feeling | NF | 41.71 | 46 |
> | Sensing-Feeling | SF | 16.82 | 19 |
> | Intuitive-Thinking | NT | 27.43 | 31 |
> | Sensing-Thinking | ST | 15.04 | 17 |
> | Totals |  | 100.00 | 113 |
>
> From the *Atlas of Type Tables* by G. P. Macdaid, M. H. McCaulley, and R. I. Kainz, 1986. Gainesville, FL: Center for Applications of Psychological Type. Used by permission.

Look at this scenario: A police investigator picks up the morning newspaper and reads about a case he has worked on the day before, and doesn't even recognize it. There may be several reasons for this, such as he couldn't give the information to the reporter, or was unable to get a copy of the report to the reporter. Here lies the rub. The reporter, being global in perspective (Intuitive), generally gets the facts in the main ballpark which, in his or her perception, is "close enough," while the Sensing cop, who knows the intimate details of the case, sees broad generalities and error in the story.

Bearing in mind, the police officer, being typically Sensing (perceiving in great detail) has a hard time understanding, from his point of view, why the reporter didn't say "at precisely 10:32 a.m., the victim descended the stairs and was accosted by the perpetrator, who inserted a seven-inch blade of a filet knife through the victim's outer clothing into a space between the sixth and seventh rib on the right side of the victim's rib cage." This only concerns the Perceptive part of the issue. Now realize that on the Judgment side of the coin, the decision-making part of cognition, they will also look at the incident from two completely different sides of the issue.

The reporter, deciding with the preferred use of the Feeling function, will look at the case with social value (Feeling), considering the fate of the victim, but also considering the human side of the crook, the family, the spouse, friends, and neighbors. While the police investigator is still trying to wash the blood off of his or her hands after the crime scene, the reporter is writing about the assailant being raised in a broken home by an alcoholic single parent who is really sorry that the child got into trouble, but he really didn't commit this crime as people think he did, and the police must have coerced a confession out of the assailant. Of course, the story the reporter is writing is a legitimate human interest story that readers are interested in. The police officer is looking at the issue through the pragmatic, objective lens (Thinking), and logically thinks the crook should be on his way to the gallows, not out on the street on bail.

Obviously, this may be somewhat of an exaggeration, but it brings home the fact that the way people generally look at things can result in real differences in how people view the world.

## Social Workers

The same differences hold true for social workers, another occupational group which may often find itself on opposite sides of an issue from the police. Since we all may look at an issue through a different lens, we have a tendency to see things from our own perspective. We are obviously not making a judgment on who may be "right or wrong" on an issue, but merely stating that our perspectives could be somewhat different.

### Table 3: Social Workers
### N = 479

|  |  | Percent | Number |
|---|---|---|---|
| Intuitive-Feeling | NF | 42.59 | 204 |
| Sensing-Feeling | SF | 21.50 | 103 |
| Intuitive-Thinking | NT | 18.58 | 89 |
| Sensing-Thinking | ST | <u>17.33</u> | <u>83</u> |
| Totals |  | 100.00 | 479 |

From the *Atlas of Type Tables* by G. P. Macdaid, M. H. McCaulley, and R. I. Kainz, 1986. Gainesville, FL: Center for Applications of Psychological Type. Used by permission.

The preference for the Feeling function in this group is over 64 percent. This means that a great majority of social workers prefer making decisions based on social value rather than pure logic. Taking the tasks of their occupation into consideration, this conclusion would appear appropriate.

During my law enforcement career, I served in a narcotics enforcement section during the early 1970s. One of my duties was training various other governmental agencies on drug identification, drug laws, and investigations. Often I was treated like an overzealous police officer by some social workers when I spoke with local and state representatives of social service departments. Some even seemed to just wait stoically until the question and answer period began and then gleefully asked if I enjoyed putting poor little teenagers who were "just smoking a little weed" into jail. They seemed to love discussing the philosophy of punishment and incarceration versus treatment. Surely I was somewhat uncomfortable around those individuals who seemed not to really understand my view of the importance strict law enforcement played in the problems of the drug culture. I'm sure they were equally uncomfortable with me as an objective, structured, law enforcement representative.

Prior to leaving my career with the department of public safety, I had occasion to work with the social service department regarding a preliminary study geared to improve the state's computer systems for dealing with battered women and domestic violence. As I talked with several social department administrators, we discussed the operations of civil divisions in sheriffs' departments. One of the managers made an unsolicited statement about how he disliked "police types" because of their apparent insensitivity. His partner, who was listening to the conversation over the office divider, chimed in with several additional comments along the same general line. I chuckled to myself as I listened to their comments about police insensitivity, they of course not realizing they were talking with a law enforcement administrator and not a computer researcher.

## Why the Conflict

People usually feel most comfortable with those we understand, can communicate well with, and whose values we seem to share. When we find ourselves in a situation where that is not the case, we have a tendency to feel uncomfortable. The others don't seem to understand our point of view. Those of us in law enforcement may feel people in the helping occupations are unrealistic, too soft, fuzzy headed, and too liberal. Even though a person is deemed innocent until proven guilty, we in law enforcement know when we arrest them they are usually guilty, right? We know the world is full of unprincipled, lying, cheating, stealing low lifes. We also know the social workers, probation officers, defense bar, and the psychologists are trying to get these degenerates back out on the street faster than we can bring them in, right? The media's point of view may not make a lot of sense to us either, as we make our judgments through pure, impersonal, and logical reasoning. No wonder law enforcement personnel appear to be cold, hard-hearted, non-compassionate human beings in the eyes of those who prefer to make their decisions through warm human insight, focusing on what they feel is best for the people involved.

Understanding various personality types of people and the varied ways they approach a problem gives us logical, rational reasons to understand why people look at issues the way they do. Jungian typology also gives us a terminology which we can apply to the different personality types. We can then use this terminology as a tool to understand the different ways we all make decisions, as well as why we make those decisions for totally different reasons and from totally different directions.

Many of us can look back on our career experiences with the helping professions and now understand why they seemed to look at issues in a completely different light than we may have viewed them. We can better understand each other's points of view and work more as a team in the criminal justice area if all sides are aware of the differences in perception and judgment.

# 11 Benefits of Understanding Personality Differences In Policing

Understanding Jungian personality theory through the use of the Myers-Briggs Type Indicator is an excellent way to help explain behaviors in the workplace. Experience has shown me, along with reasons listed by Ronald Lynch and Hobie Henson, that there are several excellent uses of Jungian typology in the police profession:

- As an aid in team building. Those who understand various personality preferences are able to recognize and accept differences in communication styles.

- It serves as a way to look at issues from different perspectives.

- It helps officers in understanding why they may feel uncomfortable in certain job situations and why they excel in some tasks and not in others.

- To be used during recruitment, not to screen out those types uncommon to law enforcement, but to help give applicants better tools to understand their own personal strengths and possible weaknesses. Additionally, it may help applicants understand the general culture they may be entering. **The Myers-Briggs Type Indicator, by itself, should not be used to screen out applicants.** There are very successful individuals of every type in all occupations.

No psychological survey alone should be used to singularly predict an individual's ability to perform a specific job. An excellent rationale is to look at the results of studies reflected in this book. Persons of all cognitive styles can perform the job of policing. Typically, as we have discussed, the majority of the people in law enforcement have a cognitive style preference for Sensing Thinking. One may assume all STs would make good police officers. Obviously this is not the case. There are bright STs and dull STs, motivated and unmotivated STs. Actually, Intuitive Feeling types, who comprise only 5% of the officers in the profession, add greatly to the quality of the occupation even though their strengths do not necessarily speak to the general tasks of the job. If MBTI results were used to screen out those who didn't fit the ST profile or to recommend to applicants they shouldn't seek a job in this profession, we would lose out on the diversity that uncommon types bring to the occupation.

As an example, an ST may bring refreshing structure and reality to a group of Ns who are intuitively dealing with an issue, while an NF may bring a global and compassionate perspective to a cold, stark, logical operation being planned by a group of STs.

In team building, it has been my experience to observe numerous instances where understanding Jungian typology and the various personality types proved to be an excellent way for explaining problems that occur with a constantly changing environment. As an example, the chief of a major police agency was an Intuitive Thinker. He had two assistants, an NT and an ST. The chief communicated well with both assistants, but spoke more of change and general conceptual operational issues, such as re-organization, with the NT. Both administrators who shared the

NT preferences would travel to various conferences and symposiums together.

Because both communicated well together in global terms, they would discuss new technology and attempt to institute change within the organization with less than optimal success. When this issue was discussed during a team building session based on Myers-Briggs cognitive styles, it became evident that the persons who favored the NT preference were too global in their applications and re-organizational issues and were missing numerous details necessary for the successful implementation of any change. Because of their familiar communication patterns and ease of understanding each other, they were inadvertently excluding the administrator with the ST preference from the critical areas of discussion, that of the actual details necessary in implementing the changes.

The NT administrators, as well as the administrator with the ST preference (the preference shared by the large majority of people charged with carrying out policy changes), agreed that the individual with the ST preference would serve as a "leavening agent" in the planning discussions to ensure a methodical, step-by-step process would be used in implementing changes within the department.

Another example of an administrator using the MBTI in the operational areas of a police organization deals with communication styles. A deputy chief, an NT, recognized the necessity of communicating in a more acceptable "tone" when issuing written directives to the sworn officers as a whole. Even though the majority of police officers are STs, they still can be affected negatively by a "curt" writing style, typical of NTs or STs. Recognizing the need to communicate in a more conciliatory tone, he would ask an individual he called "one of his few token feelers" (an NF) to look over the memoranda and make any form changes he deemed appropriate. The NF would revise the memoranda slightly, not changing the content, but only the tone of the form, to give it a more "humane" touch.

I observed another, more pragmatic, approach after a team building session with a group of police managers. One of these individuals, whose preference was ST, chose a planning committee by selecting competent individuals from each of the various personality types to serve as members. He wanted input from as many points of view as possible. He wanted Sensing Thinking types, who bring facts and present realities; Intuitive Thinking types, who bring a global, planning perspective to the table; Sensing Feeling types, who bring practical, caring solutions for the people involved; and Intuitive Feeling types, who bring innovative, insightful ideas for dealing with people issues.

Another strong benefit of knowing how different personality types function concerns understanding why some officers perform better at some tasks than others. As an example, one investigator had been in a detective bureau in a large suburban department for many years. He had been a uniform patrol officer and had risen through the ranks. He never was content or comfortable, however, in the occupation. Obviously he was able to perform the job in a satisfactory manner, but always seemed to be at loose ends; not "really fitting in" with the rest of the officers. They felt he was "kind of drifty," not sticking to the task at hand, and going off in a lot of different directions. He found his preferences were Intuitive Thinking, with his dominant being Intuition. After an explanation of these preferences, he began to understand why he was uncomfortable around Sensing types, why they didn't accept him, and why he didn't quite fit in. He was able to transfer into a job which was research-based, dealing with computers, intelligence data, and special projects, and became a strong contributor to the investigative process. He has since gone on to graduate school with the intentions of becoming a counseling psychologist.

Another example deals with much the same situation with a patrol officer in another large city. He had been on the road for several years, enjoyed being a cop, but was very uncomfortable with the confrontations with motorists and some other, less pleasant duties connected with traffic accidents. Even though he was talented in his ability to deal with people, he was thinking of leaving the occupation. In looking at his MBTI results, he found that he preferred NF, the cognitive style of only five percent of police officers. Understanding this, he sought and obtained a transfer into the photographic and media unit. There he performed in an outstanding manner.

Administrators who are Intuitive Thinking types and Sensing Thinking types make decisions using analytical, objective, logical criteria. They typify most police officers since NT and ST are the predominant cognitive styles in the profession. They do recognize, however, that the Feeling types, the NFs and SFs, in their departments are different from themselves and the average police officer.

The reason STs and NTs seem to get along well with each other is that both share the same method of making decisions that of impersonal, analytical logic (Thinking). They do, however, have a difference in Perception. The reason this difference in Perception is not so obvious is because Perception is the taking in of information prior to making a decision. This taking in of information is usually non-verbal. The difference in Sensing and Intuition can, however, be recognized through action. As an example of this difference, typically NTs are more global and future-oriented, looking down the road, and not necessarily as grounded in detail as the STs. Hence, they are usually not as good at remembering detail in the present sense.

The following deputy chief, an NT, commented:

> *We were riding through the district and there was a call about a robbery of a convenience store that had just taken place. I was driving and my partner said, "Come on, we gotta go to this convenience store." I said to him, "We're not going to catch him by going up there. He's long gone from there." I said, "Let's drive by the other convenience store in our district and maybe we'll get lucky"... We drove up a side street,*

*turned the headlights off, and drove down to the cross street, and as we got to the intersection, the guy came running out with a shotgun...We bailed out of the car and chased him and caught the prick. It turned out there was a car up the street a ways where there was another guy, the lookout, with a driver. It seemed they had done three other very vicious stick-ups. If Bob had been driving we would have gone to the convenience store that was robbed because that's what you do.*

This is an example of global thinking, or thinking ahead, not necessarily remaining tied to the detail of the moment. The NT captain commented that he had never been very good with remembering names, license plates, or detail. He had never found any stolen cars. He commented that the only way he would know a car was stolen was "if it ran into me on the street." He knows he is different from the other commanders around the city. Each morning when the other captains report to duty, they go through all of the incident reports from the night before to see what went on in their district. This chief, when he was a captain, assumed if something important occurred during the night watch he would be told about it.

Paying attention to detail or not being generally good at detail can be the primary difference between STs and NTs. The reason, however, NTs and STs don't usually see the difference is that one cannot necessarily see how a person is taking in information, i.e., using the Perceiving function of S or N. On the other hand, when the Judgment functions of Thinking or Feeling are used, they are readily observable. When a decision has been made about a matter, the Thinking type will recite the pros and cons with a critical analysis of the facts. The Feeling type will describe the impact on people and stress the human values that contributed to the decision. STs, the predominant type in law enforcement, share the same Judgment function as the NTs. Hence, they may not easily recognize their SN differences.

Understanding the benefits of how we best function is reflected in a detective bureau where one ST and one NT were teamed up in a crime scene search group. The NT would do a crime scene search, finding evidence, mapping locations, bagging up evidence, and other detail work, and invariably, the ST would come along and find additional evidence missed by the NT. The NT's preferred method of Perception caused him to skim over the scene and miss important detail.

In a recent instance, an NT officer was asked to design an occupational physical testing course for recruits and veteran officers to substitute for Cooper Physical Standards Measurements as these standards were coming under some scrutiny for not being job related. The NT designed a complex, comprehensive course on a large white board, drafted the specifications, and began to seek out the materials and labor to complete the job. His ST supervisor asked for a comprehensive written document detailing exactly what he was doing and how he intended to accomplish the job. The NT, hearing this, seemed to lose the "wind out of his sails." To him, he was moving right along past the need to write about it and was busy getting the job done, "skipping steps," as NTs often do. The ST was just asking for a detailed explanation and covering all of the bases, as STs do. The NT had to stop and cover all of the bases prior to continuing.

As another example of cognitive differences, a recruit was continually forgetting small items such as a specific part of a uniform needed for the day, or a tag, or PT equipment. He was at a loss trying to understand why he was doing this, as he usually had a good memory for things in the past. When questioned as to what he did prior to coming to the police academy, he stated he was a research assistant part time at the university he attended, enjoyed reading history books, and had graduated with a political science degree. He enjoyed art, drama, and other more intellectual pursuits. These traits are typical of an individual who prefers to take in and process information intuitively. When he entered the highly structured, life of a police academy, he struggled with the detail required to succeed. Additionally, the very issue of being in a somewhat stressful academy situation affects individuals' abilities to concentrate and pay attention to detail. When he understood these issues and cognitive differences, he began to keep a structured daily list of what he had to do for the next day. He didn't like the list as he felt it was a "crutch," but it enabled him to make it successfully through the academy. When he graduated, he was also armed with the knowledge of what the profession required and what it would be necessary for him to do to fit in and be successful.

## Cognitive Learning Styles of Police

As we are aware, over 65 percent of all law enforcement officers prefer to take in information and process it through their five senses rather than through intuition, which means they are "bound in reality." Additionally, 85 percent prefer to make decisions through pure logic. Other personality measures that look at how police function also reflect these same general results. As we have seen in the past, those in our profession tend to be practical and analytical and are seldom wrong with the facts. We are naturally brief and businesslike and if forced to choose between tact and truthfulness, will usually chose truthfulness.

### Teaching Cultural Awareness

In view of the above, two important considerations arise, one when teaching cultural awareness issues and the second when dealing with citizen problems, particularly those from minority communities. First, the message presented needs to be factual, pragmatic, realistic, and practical. Officers need to know why they have to learn how to deal with differences. The law enforcement community is 85 percent white male in this country, and the demographics of the majority of departments, with few exceptions in large cities, reflect these statistics. The cognitive style of making decisions through objective logic does not necessarily emphasize a value for issues of compassion, empathy, congeniality, and the rationale of valuing diversity for the sake of social issues and humanity alone. They are primarily concerned with truth, justice, ethics, and fairness. Law enforcement officers need to know why it is important for them to spend time learning about these issues. In our profession, the appeal needs to be to the head, not the heart. Understanding the importance of becoming culturally competent has to have a rational basis, such as making their jobs safer by knowing how others react, or gaining the respect of the changing community, or understanding the powerful force the minority community is becoming in our cities.

STs learn best through discussions with each other, performing special paper/pencil exercises, role plays, and case studies, as well as interactions with the instructor. They do not learn well listening to lectures or playing games that have no rational basis in their minds. The use of case studies and discussions affords them the opportunity to express themselves and contribute their experience and points of view.

As you can see, the common types in law enforcement, the Sensing Thinking types and the Intuitive Thinking types, the less common Sensing Feeling types, and the least common Intuitive Feeling types can all perform the job of policing. All of the various types bring differing strengths to the occupation. The more we understand individuals and their various preferences and attitudes, the closer we can come to understanding the profession. It is obvious that the attitudes and behaviors of police officers are not simple phenomena. Personality and behavior are extremely complicated. The MBTI gives us an excellent opportunity to observe the complex world of police behavior in a completely different light.

# 12   Watching Type At Work

During my thirty-two-plus years in the law enforcement profession, I have had an incredible number of opportunities to watch type at work in the world of policing. From individual interactions to those in classes of recruits, type becomes very evident if one watches for it.

We all know that type certainly isn't everything and that personality is extremely complex to say the least. However, that said, students of type continually see its effect in everyday life. Take the example of recognizing differences in groups of police officer recruits.

## The Police Academy Setting

During 1996, I had the opportunity to administer the Myers-Briggs Type Indicator to some four hundred and fifty recruits in a large Southwestern police academy. The MBTI was used to help them understand the police culture and the communication styles of the majority of law enforcement officers in contrast to the general public. It was also used to help them understand differences in cultural communication and how many other cultures communicate differently than police officers. The results of this study reflected the general type distribution characteristic of other research into cognitive styles of police in the past twenty years. In this study, the vast majority of recruits (over 78%) preferred ST as a cognitive style. In each class, there were no more than six or seven NFs and SFs. As I was instructing on communication skills or cultural awareness subjects, their comments and learning styles were very true to type. The vast majority of questions and discussions revolved around a critical analysis of the subject matter. The many groups of approximately forty recruits per class had been together for ten to fourteen weeks when I had the opportunity to spend several days with them, and consequently they knew each other well.

When we were discussing type after taking the instrument, I would ask those NFs and SFs if they felt they were different from the rest of the recruits in their specific class or general recruit population at the academy. All stated openly in class that they had felt somewhat different from most of the instructors and other recruits. Additionally, some stated that they had often wondered if this profession was the one for them or if they had mis-selected policing, recognizing that their preferences in communication and looking at the world differed from those of the majority of their classmates. When asked how they were different, many would state "I think I am more people-oriented, more compassionate, than most others in this class." Other Feeling types would nod in agreement. One male NF recruit stated "I think I am more compassionate than the rest of these slugs," to the laughter of the rest of the class. During these open discussions, classmates recognized they knew each other quite well and agreed with the assessments of their fellow recruits. Many of the STs in the group also recognized that the Feeling types were more friendly and people-oriented and seemed to be more interactive in a friendly sort of way. The classes also recognized that the Thinking types were those that personified the general culture of policing, while the Feeling types were those that may have an advantage in dealing with the community because of their obvious skills in relating to people on a more personal basis.

These discussions were very revealing and the personality characteristics were easily recognizable to the class. You do not need a formal assessment instrument such as the MBTI or the Law Enforcement Type Sorter* to recognize preferences in people. A member of a class of forty-three sat up in the top row of the graduated risers in the classroom. Throughout the first part of the presentation, he had asked very intellectual, probing questions, and critically assessed information being presented to him and his classmates about communication, culture, and different value systems. At no time in the morning session did he smile or socially interact with the rest of the class. His interactions and conversations with other class members were direct, structured discussions with critical analysis of the facts of what was being presented. The MBTI reflected his preference as ST. After he received the results of the assessment, he raised his hand and stated "I don't really believe the results of this instrument. I don't think I am an ST, I think I am an NF." The rest of his classmates looked back and up at him quizzically. He then said seriously, "I really think I am a warm, friendly, compassionate sort of a guy." With that comment, his classmates burst out laughing. They did not believe his self-assessment at all. To the rest of the class, his actions throughout the training period reflected a strong preference for functioning as an ST. He seemed very surprised that he wasn't perceived as he felt he really was, an NF, but was perceived as he behaved, an ST.

During these class interactions, numerous student recruits with SF and NF preferences approached me after class and thanked me for giving them the insight through the MBTI that they were not crazy, or inadequate, or wrong. Many had really believed they were in the wrong profession or that something was

---

* Instrument designed by author to identify Jungian cognitive styles. Published by Leadership Inc., Scottsdale, AZ.

wrong with them. The explanation of type and preferences gave them new understanding of their own and their classmates' behavior. They also stated they more fully understood the profession and the police culture and believed they would be able to function better on the street because of the information. All of the groups of recruits stated they had gained new insights into how the majority of officers prefer to function in the world of law enforcement, and particularly how these differences can affect communication with members of other diverse communities.

## Surveys of What the Community Wants in Law Enforcement Officers

There have been numerous studies and surveys of citizens throughout the United States to ascertain what they expect from their law enforcement officers. In 1997, the Peace Officers' Standards and Training Board in Arizona conducted a survey of citizens from fifty-six various diverse communities throughout Arizona with surprising results.

The citizens assumed that officers could make an arrest, shoot the gun straight, drive a patrol car, and enforce the law. This was their primary request: "I want my officers to communicate with us...talk to us and wave when you pass by. Do not drive or walk by just as if we weren't there." Their second most common desire was for police officers to show compassion. They wanted police to act as if they really cared about the job and their role in the community. These two initial wants from the community are somewhat different than most police officers expected. They also reinforced the thought that the communities desire communication skills from the officers that serve them.

Recruits and officers both must realize the importance of communication and a cordial interaction with the public. Officers and recruits are often urged to watch those officers that are more successful on the street. Usually those that do the best in working with informants and sources and solve the most cases have learned to look at the world from an SF or NF orientation.

## Recruiting and Communication

In another large police agency, the commander of the recruiting function rotated into the position, bringing with him those he had worked well with in past assignments. The commander of the recruiting bureau reviewed all of the files and made the final decision on recruits coming into the academy. In this situation, the importance and value of understanding type at work is again reflected.

One commander, who had an ST preference, recruited a second in command whom he had worked well with in the past and who was also an ST. They were closely involved in the recruiting, interviewing, and supervision of the recruiting process and had the final decision on who the successful candidates would be. They also assisted in the oral board selection that interviewed and tested the recruits. During the two years that both of these individuals headed the recruiting function, the vast majority of recruits entering the academy were STs, as one would expect. However, STs were hired at an even higher rate that one would usually find in a general police population. As a matter of fact, ninety percent of the recruits coming through the academy during that period of time were STs and NTs.

Several years later, another commander, whose preference was SF, rotated into the recruiting function. He brought with him another individual to be his second in command who was, not surprisingly, because of communications preferences, another SF. There was a noticeable increase in SFs and NFs coming to the academy under this hiring group. For the next several years, NFs and SFs comprised twenty-five percent of the academy class, rather than the previous ten percent. This reflects an interesting validation of the presumption that you communicate best with those with whom you share the same cognitive styles. The SF and NF recruits seemed to be making it through the interview process in greater numbers than before. Interestingly enough, many veteran police officers were heard to complain that the recruits coming out of the academy were "soft and too people-oriented" and would get hurt on the street.

**Officers will tend to gravitate to those functions that best validate and support their strengths.**

The larger the police agency, the more the varied tasks of policing are assigned to specific commands or groups of officers. As we know, a large agency will have functions such as Community Relations, S.W.A.T. hostage negotiators, Traffic Enforcement, Motors (as traffic officers on motorcycles are called), School Resource Officers, Personnel and Administration, Neighborhood Patrol Officers, D.A.R.E. and Gang Resistance Education and Training Officers, Patrol, Narcotics, Homicide, Sex Crimes, and so on.

Invariably, you will find a majority of a specific cognitive style preference in each of the above working groups. Even when teaching a group of recruits for the first time about type and its function in everyday life, they can easily guess the cognitive preference of the majority of officers working in a specific task group. For example, the majority of officers in a formal community relations function are Feeling types. The class guesses Feeling for that group as well as School Resource Officers, D.A.R.E., and Neighborhood Policing officers. Not surprisingly, they will strongly call out "T!" when I point to Motorcycle Traffic Officers, S.W.A.T., or the Drug Enforcement Bureau. To further validate that assumption, I had the opportunity to administer the Myers-Briggs Type Indicator to a group of forty-five Gang Resistance Education and Training officers from a variety of departments around the United States. The students preferred Feeling to Thinking at a ratio of three to one.

Another example of similar types grouping by policing function was seen at a day long course on hate crimes held by a major law enforcement agency. Leaders and members of various visible minority populations, as well as members of the Gay and Lesbian community, were invited to a discussion of several questions such as "How do hate crimes affect your specific community?" and "How can your community help the police in identifying and solving hates crimes?" The forty or so attendees from this police department were members of assaults, homicide, and property crimes details, as well as officers from the community relations bureau. Those individuals from the investigative units were predominantly Thinking types, and those from community relations were predominantly Feeling types. When the officers entered the room and sat at the U-shaped conference table, they sat together as a unit, assaults with assaults, community relations with community relations, and homicide with homicide. Watching from the corner of the room, one could observe type and other group dynamics at work, from the questions asked by the various groups of police officers to their reactions to comments by the panel members of the various diverse groups. The Feeling types discussed people issues and the Thinking types discussed statistics, figures, and issues and concerns based on objective criteria. The Thinking types challenged the speakers on statistical and analytical grounds, while the Feeling types discussed issues from a personal point of view.

The climax of the meeting occurred when the last member of the panel to speak decided not to comment on the designated questions but to bring up a high profile shooting incident that had occurred the previous year. This panel member commented about supposed police misconduct and liability, as well as other emotionally charged issues, that had long ago been resolved legally in favor of the police action in the situation. The investigators in the group rationally and critically argued about mis-statements of fact by the panel member and challenged his comments and stance, while the community relations groups listened to his comments and let the speaker continue on without interruption until he was finished. As the room became somewhat emotionally charged, the meeting and presentations were brought to a close and the speakers thanked for their participation.

The discussion that had taken place clearly indicated the differences in cognitive styles, the Thinking types still arguing errors in fact, while the Feeling types discussing the effect the shooting had on various minority communities and the challenge to build dialogue. This interchange not only demonstrated differences in type, but differences between the police culture and other cultures as far as communication context is concerned, which will be discussed in the next chapter.

# 13 Cognitive Styles of Police And The Changing Cultural Community

Those in the law enforcement profession tend to communicate differently than the majority of the public they serve. Many studies involving communication styles would tend to reflect that Lower Context Cultures characteristically speak in ST terms, while those not in law enforcement positions in Higher Context Cultures tend to speak in NT, SF, and NF terms.

As we have discussed throughout this book, the great majority of law enforcement officers prefer to take in information and process it through Sensing rather than Intuition, which means they are "bound in reality and pay attention to the here and now." We also know that at least eighty percent of officers prefer to make decisions through Thinking, using logical, impersonal analysis. Other personality measures with police populations from around the world seem to reflect the same results.

During a trip to the Far East and Singapore, I had the opportunity to speak to several groups of police officers with the Singapore State Police as well as officers with Singapore Airlines (S.A.T.S.) Police. Even though they were all representative of a culture that is Asian by definition, they were still police officers performing the same tasks as police officers from other parts of the world.

The preferences of over one hundred officers from Singapore reflected a three to one preference for ST, the same ratio as officers in most police departments in the United States.

As we know, the general descriptors of law enforcement officers with ST or NT cognitive preferences are:

| | | |
|---|---|---|
| Concrete | Decisive | Traditional |
| Practical | Impersonal | Matter-of-fact |
| Observant | Structured | Precise |
| Logical | Factual | Pragmatic |
| Systematic | Detached | Direct |

Individuals in the law enforcement profession tend to speak in direct, practical, and analytical terms and are seldom wrong about the facts. They are naturally brief and businesslike and if forced to choose between tact and truthfulness, will usually choose truthfulness. Police will communicate in an ST manner the vast majority of the time. Members of other cultures usually communicate more subjectively and personally. We can compare and contrast various cultural styles in context and their significance in communicating and interacting with the police. This ST culture is reinforced through the media, particularly television where one can pick up a TV schedule and see shows advertised such as *Cops, Highway Patrol, The Canadian Mounties,* and *Dangerous Police Chases,* all action-oriented depictions of police work.

## Characteristics of Culture

We are all individuals, as type theory states, but we also share certain common ways of taking in information and making decisions. The same can be said about our cultural context. Each person that is related to, or comes from, a specific culture shares, to one extent or another, characteristics of that culture. As we know through research, cultural characteristics and how to behave in a culture are handed down through the generations by people of that culture. As there are individual differences among people who share the same personality type, so there are individual differences within a cultural context. People, however, tend to behave as the majority of those from the same culture behave. With that understanding in mind, let us begin by discussing the term "Context of Culture" and characteristics that researchers in the communication field have discovered.

## The Context of Culture

The context-of-culture approach has been widely recognized in the communication field for years, but has not been extensively used as a way of helping to understand the police culture and its interaction with various minority cultures, particularly in the United States. Context, among other definitions, refers to the ways information is handled in communicating in a specific cultural group. Language carries a message, but various cultures interpret the meaning of the words and the way they are delivered differently. Communication context considers the relationship between the sender and the receiver; how the language is used; and the body language involved, i.e., posturing, gesturing, and facial expressions.

Various cultures can be placed along a continuum, from the lowest context, where words comprise most of the message, to the highest context, where words, emotion, and emphasis all combine into the message one wants to send. Because one culture is lower and another higher on the continuum does not reflect that one is better than another. Edward T. Hall, a well known sociologist and an expert in communication, commented often on the importance of understanding the context of a culture. Let us look at Lower Context Cultures and Higher Context Cultures.

## Lower Context Cultures

The cultures lower on the continuum are typically English, German, Swiss, Dutch, and Scandinavian. This is also the context of the police culture.

## Verbal communication

Verbal communication seems to reflect the following values and methods of passing information from one to another. Words send most of the message and are extremely important. Specifics, details, and facts, as well as explicit meanings, are important parts of this communication structure. The words and ways of communicating are more structured and direct with less emotion involved in the process. Remember Jack Webb in Dragnet? "Just the facts, ma'am."

People are usually concerned more with the who, what, where, when, how, and why of issues rather than form. Linear thinking is structured and direct. The primary language spoken in the U.S. is English, which is a lower context language. The structure of words sends most of the message. Additionally, German, Dutch, and the Scandinavian languages employ this direct communication style.

There is a low use of non-verbal elements. The message is carried more by words than with other non-verbal means. The verbal messages are explicit. Contexts in which verbal messages are spoken are much less important than the words.

The verbal message is direct; things are spelled out exactly. Communication is seen as a way of exchanging information, ideas, and opinions.

Disagreement is depersonalized. One withdraws from conflict with another and gets on with the task. The focus is on rational solutions, not personal ones. One can be explicit about another's bothersome behavior and comment on it.

Generally speaking, Lower Context behavioral traits can be broadly equated with general North American cultural values. One may be surprised to learn that the majority of Americans draw their ancestry from lower context cultures, primarily German. Ask any group of people at a training session to share their ancestral heritage and, even though most will share a combination of backgrounds, the most common will be German, English, Scandinavian, or Irish. As we know, the largest groups of immigrants to this country, as the culture originally formed, were from lower context cultures such as Germany, northern Europe, and England.

The top ten ancestry groups in the United States are:

1. German
2. Irish
3. English
4. African
5. Italian
6. Mexican
7. French
8. Polish
9. American Indian
10. Dutch

## Higher Context Cultures

As we move along the continuum, we find higher context cultures such as French, Italian, and Arab and other Middle Eastern cultures. The highest context cultures are Asian, Hispano/Latino, African, Black American, and Native American.

## Verbal Communications

In higher context cultures, words send only part of the message. Words are much less important than the context of the message. The *process* of communication seems to be just as important as the words used.

Emotion, posturing, and gesturing may be part of the communication process. There is usually less direct eye contact, or deferred eye contact. The communication is more verbose and less direct.

In Higher Context Cultures, the process of communication may bury the implicit meanings of the words used or the intended message. The message that is spoken has to be understood in the whole context of the conversation or discussion.

There is a higher use of non-verbal elements: voice tone, facial expression, gesture, eye movement. The verbal message is implicit; context is more important than words. The spoken message is indirect with a person preferring to talk around a point, embellishing the point for effect.

Communication is seen as an art form, a way to engage someone. Disagreement is personalized. People tend to be more sensitive to conflict expressed in another's non-verbal cues. Often conflict must be solved before work can continue, or must be avoided because it may be personally threatening.

The communication patterns of Asians, Hispano/Latinos, Africans, and Native Americans tend to be more complex than lower context cultural communication. In Asian culture and American Indian culture, silence is also a form of complex communication. Hispano/Latino and Black American cultures can be more vocal and emotional, with less concern for direct meanings. This is true even if an individual from the culture has been in the U.S. for generations. In African and Black American cultures, use of expressive voice and language is highly valued. Ask any law enforcement officer what typically occurs when they stop a car in Hispano/Latino or African-American neighborhoods. In these neighborhoods, the people come out of their homes and gather around to see what is going on. They are interested in one thing, information, and they are often not quiet in demanding it.

While teaching cultural awareness to a group of police officers, the matter of more expressive and louder speech came up in reference to some members of the Black American culture. One Black officer stood up and commented, "When my wife and I are having a rather strong discussion, there is a lot of volume and expressive force involved. The average White cop may think we are having an argument and are about to hurt one another. I want him or her to know that is not the case. We are just discussing. I don't want him to rush in and arrest one of us."

The higher context culture often places a high value on the extended family. Minority cultures may feel powerless at times and will act to protect themselves. The conversational level may be louder than in other neighborhoods, with other *machismo* behavior or emotion displayed. The police represent power and it is typical for some young males to try to challenge that power in one way or another. Often power is the greater theme in these interactions, rather than race. Race is often only used as an excuse. A Black officer may get even more of a challenge than some White officers in a Black neighborhood. The issues of extended family and emotional, loud, or complex communication can be contrasted to the police mission of keeping the peace, calming everyone down, and restoring order. Order may exist even though it may not appear so to the typical Lower Context Anglo with an ST preference for taking in information and making decisions.

To help officers understand other cultures' concern for extended family members and own race, we discuss how we feel when an officer is shot down or is hurt in an accident. Even if we don't know that officer, we still feel concern for that person and will band together to express solidarity for, and to protect, that person. Individuals whose cultures involve extended family structure feel the same concern when a member of their culture or race gets into any sort of trouble with the police.

## Immigrant Information

If one were to look at the immigration information, one could see a vast difference since the 1940s. At that time approximately 70% of immigrants came from Europe. Compare that to the countries of origin for immigrants today.

### 1990 Immigrants

| | |
|---|---|
| Latin America-Caribbean | 46.0% |
| Asia | 37.0% |
| Europe | 17.0% |

### 1992 Immigrants

| | |
|---|---|
| Mexico | 22.0% |
| Vietnam | 8.0% |
| Filipinos | 6.3% |
| Soviet Union | 4.5% |
| Dominican Republic | 4.3% |
| China | 4.0% |

### United States Population Projections
Estimates based on 1990 Census Data

| | 1990 | 2050 |
|---|---|---|
| Anglo | 76% | 52% |
| African American | 12% | 16% |
| Latino | 9% | 22% |
| Asian | 3% | 10% |

### Foreign Born Populations in Selected Cities

| | | | |
|---|---|---|---|
| Miami | 60% | San Francisco | 19% |
| Union City, NJ | 55% | New York City | 12% |
| Los Angeles | 21% | Chicago | 7% |

The concern for understanding the importance of differences in culture and communication and the role of the police in society is not new. Negative attitudes held by police regarding race and culture were evident and noted by police researchers in the early 1900s. In 1929, one noted researcher, Charles Simon, stated there was a belief held by many police officers "that the immigrant population was composed of the mentally and morally unfit of Europe." There was little or no tolerance for immigrants on the part of police, even though many of the officers were recent immigrants themselves. Today, some Americans are heard to make statements such as "they take all our jobs, impose their culture, and don't even try to assimilate."

As has been emphasized, the importance of understanding type as an important factor in styles of communication, and interconnecting it into values of higher context and lower context intercultural communication, can go a long way in helping law enforcement officers to better understand and do their jobs.

# 14 Cognitive Styles and Teaching In The Law Enforcement Profession

As educators and trainers, we all have our favorite methods of teaching. Our teaching styles are a reflection of our cognitive style. Our success or lack of success often lies in our failure to understand the favorite cognitive processes of our audience.

I have had many consultants and trainers comment to me and swear they will "never try to teach a bunch of cops again." Many consultants and trainers struggle with law enforcement audiences or engineers, for that matter, and may rate the students as too serious, critical and cynical, not very interactive or friendly, not willing to have fun and play games. They may see them as seldom smiling and having a hard time enjoying themselves. They may see the audience as uncooperative and swear never to teach a law enforcement audience again. Usually the problem doesn't lie with the audience itself, but with the fact that the teaching style of the consultant or trainer is not compatible with that of the students. In this situation, the very interaction of the group suffers.

As an example, an NF professor may approach teaching through creative writing exercises or a process utilizing self expressive strategies, metaphors, and symbolic representations. The use of visual and performing arts as well as meditation may be employed. The teacher enjoys the presentations and the pleasure of teaching from his or her favorite place. Often the directions given by NF teachers, as well as NT teachers, can be somewhat general, broad, and perhaps even vague. Details and specifics are not usually high on the lists of important issues with Intuitives. As NFs, we enjoy our favorite teaching style and often miss the apparent struggle that students may be having with the material and our teaching methods because of the power we have as the head of the classroom.

Several police/professor stories come to mind. A large Southwestern police department has numerous groups, or cohorts, attending a Master's in Educational Leadership program at a local university. The cohort members range from officers recently out of the academy to assistant chiefs. The professors from the School of Education, many of whom are NFs, are finding some challenges with these groups of students. I have the pleasure of acting as a coordinator of the cohorts.

One professor, a strong NF, counseled with me at the end of a course. She felt she had not done as well as she usually does with her own students in education. During the final class session after the final was handed in, she was used to having most, if not all, of the students in her class come up and chat, tell her how much they enjoyed the class, and generally socialize. She commented that about half of the police cohort students just got up, handed in the final and left. She was concerned that she had not gained their confidence.

I mentioned the issue of ST being the prevalent cognitive style of police, and that they were probably just thinking "OK, now I have to think about the next class" in a logical manner and just moving on. Probably less than cordial behavior, but doubtfully signifying anything negative about the instructor. I confirmed that by speaking to two of the students she mentioned had left without speaking to her. They both said "I'm sorry, I just wasn't thinking along those lines. She was an excellent teacher. I was just moving on in my mind."

Several other students would call and complain "she doesn't give specific instructions" or "he keeps changing the requirements on us" or "he isn't clear enough and just says to go ahead and anything we do on that subject matter will be fine." This would appear to be a typical ST cry for structure and direction.

When I speak about type and its importance in the classroom, not only do I speak to the professors, I also speak to students and explain the cognitive styles of various professors and the challenges inherent in these styles for the students. It may not be comfortable for them to just "go with the flow" when the directions are not as specific as they would like or the subject matter is not presented in a manner that is as logical or structured as they would like. I mention to the students that as teachers themselves after the course of study is over, they will also be faced with the issues of understanding their students. I speak to their own ST styles and how they may have to loosen up and modify and adapt for students, especially if they are teaching in the areas of drama or the arts.

As we all know, it may be difficult for us to learn in ways that are different from our own cognitive styles. To reinforce the points of cognitive styles, I come into a classroom of STs with a cassette player and tell them I am going to play some meditation music, ask them to put their heads down on the desk and take themselves back in memory to a favorite place in their childhood where they felt safe and secure, and to go to that place for ten minutes. I tell them that afterwards I am going to ask them to draw a self expressive, symbolic representation of that place. During these instructions, there is giggling from the majority of the students and outright guffaws from several. I then explain differences in teaching styles and that each style accomplishes certain missions, including the benefits of the NF style I have just employed. Of course, they know me as an analytical ENTJ and know that the demonstrated teaching method was not really my preferred style.

## Keys in Teaching Law Enforcement Officers

When we look at the specifics of cognitive styles within the law enforcement profession, we can make some assumptions as to the best way to present classroom material and get the message across when teaching in this profession. When teaching cultural awareness, gender issues, or any other subject for that matter, the following learning strategies, structure and environment should be used as often as possible.

When teaching a general audience of individuals in the law enforcement profession, the instructor can assume that the vast majority (80%) are looking at the issues being taught with a Thinking cognitive style. They are using a critical eye and have favored methods of making decisions about the material. As you look over the audience, they will be generally serious. They will usually not be socially interacting with each other as do many other groups. They are ready to filter the information through their logical and critical lenses.

STs and NTs learn best through material focusing on facts and logic. They like to look at objective criteria and want to know what is expected. The goals and objectives of the class or training session should be up front and accurate, and should include instructions on how to do things.

STs and NTs focus on efficient reasoning, both deductive (parts to whole) and inductive (whole to parts). They will critically argue issues to the point of splitting hairs. They focus on rationality and practicality. They like to demonstrate proficiency as well as compare and contrast issues. They want to know what, when, where, why, and lastly, the people part of the equation, who.

Focusing on presenting to the cognitive style of the greatest number of people in the audience does not mean that the rest of the SFs and NFs are being ignored. They will move right along with the STs and NTs, bringing in the people issues and subjective data for discussion.

The best way to get the message across to STs and NTs is to tell them why the subject matter is important to them and their profession.

They enjoy writing exercises and test items such as:

- True/false
- Multiple choice
- Fill-in-the-blank
- Circle the correct answer

They also enjoy case studies and discussions about current issues that affect them. They enjoy an opportunity to speak to leadership about issues involving supervision. They like to demonstrate specific skills and give specific reports. They like debates as well as panel and group discussions. They enjoy taking current issues and events and discussing alternatives. They even learn through lecture, which has fallen on disrepute of late in favor of interactive exercises.

They will look for specific direction and guidance. Typically STs want directions to be very specific, concise, and correct. They will find mistakes in dates, times, places, etc., quickly. They are into detail. They like assignments that tell them how many pages, single or double spaced, what size font, cover sheet or not, and styles of presentation.

The next several pages reflect a successful methodology in teaching a group of ST and NT law enforcement officers one of the toughest subjects in the profession, that of cultural awareness.

## Teaching Cultural Awareness to Law Enforcement Officers

A real and specific example of the importance of cognitive style in teaching has been the apparent lack of success of cultural awareness training programs in the law enforcement profession until just recently. The methodology successfully used in teaching cultural awareness can be used in any other facilitation or classroom study with law enforcement audiences.

Those in the areas of training materials development, training, and consulting have been traditionally NF or SF. Their methodologies stressed understanding diversity from a valuing point of view. The various differences were depicted as layers in a cake, as slices of a pie, a varied view of a rainbow. The methodologies and objectives of those programs, typically developed for private corporations, do not work with law enforcement audiences. What was not taken into account were cognitive styles of the sender and of the receiver, as well as the power police individuals have over citizens in their daily duties and their value systems.

If one designs programs from their most favored process and tries to implement them with individuals having completely opposite cognitive preferences, success is doubtful, to say the least. With law enforcement, the following methodologies are tried and true and have proven successful with even the most difficult of subject matter.

- The classroom information presented needs to be factual, realistic, concrete, and practical. I stress the importance of pragmatic rationale for these classes at the on-set. The Thinking cognitive style of making decisions through analytical logic does not key on issues of compassion, empathy, congeniality; the rationale of valuing diversity for the sake of social value; or valuing humanity over truth, justice, ethics, and fairness. This doesn't mean that officers do not have or share qualities of tenderness, compassion, or empathy; they just don't usually show them. Police need to know pragmatically, logically, and objectively why it's important for them to spend time learning about these issues. With this profession, the appeal needs to be directed to the head, not the heart. Understanding the importance of becoming culturally competent needs to have a rational basis such as making their jobs safer or gaining the respect of the community.

- Trainers need to be committed to these issues and must be willing to dedicate time to personally expand their knowledge in these complex areas. The need to study human behavior, keep current on new research, and study trends is paramount to success.

- In planning, trainers need to be acutely aware of what each exercise is designed to accomplish, and be willing to adjust and insure the objectives of the exercises are met. Each activity should be structured to build on the preceding ones.

- Place the attendees in groups of four, five, or six. Less than four and they may decide not to participate. Groups of more than six can also divide and decide not to participate. Even the toughest group of police officers will contribute if allowed an opportunity. If students are in a "seats facing forward" classroom or auditorium, the instructor is set up as "The Expert." Those sitting in the audience have several choices in addition to learning which include sitting it out or trying to trip up the instructor, the latter sometimes being an entertaining option. Using a lecture method of instruction with this cognitive style does not optimize learning in these courses.

- Trust in the intellectual level of the group. Place attendees in teams to facilitate discussions. The rationale of placing attendees in teams of four, five, or six allows the facilitator to ask the group to consider questions or issues that are complex. Those in the group who react immediately to an emotional or value-laden issue can be balanced by those that will give the issues considerable thought and speak later. Remember, even though attendees may not state it directly, participants are listening and may modify their own biases and thoughts from what they hear.

- Even though the groups may come from the same department, one may be very receptive while the next can be difficult. Understand that this is generally the rule and not the exception. In fact, you may feel rather "beat up" at the conclusion of one session, while others really seem to click to your satisfaction.

- Don't be concerned if you fail to keep to your course outline or schedule. The discussions may become involved. The discussions between the group participants are an important learning phase of the course. Make sure, however, the discussions are relevant to the topic. Some venting may be appropriate, but if the participants wander too far, bring them back on course.

- Sometimes exercises may "flop." Be assured it rarely is the result of your style, but in the composition of the group and their willingness (or lack thereof) to discuss the issues. If you get little reaction from one exercise, move on to the next without much comment. You will soon get back on track. Remember, some exercises that work well with some groups may not affect others in quite the same way. Forge ahead! At least they are thinking, which is what you want them to do.

- Don't use numerical grading systems or specific critiques in these courses if you can avoid it. We put too much stock on percentages or numbers as a measure of success. If the administration insists on numerical rating as a performance measure of the instructor, please put them in perspective. You may wish to rate the presenter's skills in facilitation and the material or subject matter presented separately, allowing some venting against the material, not the instructor. Teaching cultural awareness is called emotion negative training. You are asking people to examine some strongly held beliefs, some of which may be reinforced on the street in a negative way every day. As a general rule, you may not get ratings as high as in other classes you have been teaching. Percentages and scores have no relation to success in issues of this nature.

- Attendees should be engaged in active dialogue and exercises during most of the training sessions. The small group setting gives them the opportunity to continually interact with each other. They learn best through discussions with each other, performing various pencil/paper exercises, and inter-action with the instructor. Much of the learning in courses of this type takes place through the interaction between students. No matter what someone says about an issue or how pragmatically they may disagree, they will hear and consider other points of view from their peers, which is all we can ask.

- The instructor's role is that of a facilitator rather than a teacher, calling upon various groups and individuals for comments and opinions as often as possible. This keeps attention focused on the subject and stimulates thought, and affords the attendees an opportunity to express themselves. The use of case studies and role plays also affords them opportunities to contribute their experience and points of view.

- Lastly, we highly recommend placing emphasis on the experience, ability, and intellect of the officers themselves in discussing community concerns and the police response to these issues. There is a vast amount of untapped knowledge within the law enforcement community in both sworn and civilian employees. Give them an opportunity to express themselves and become a part of this process. They are the ones that have the most to gain and probably the most to lose.

## Facilitation Skills

Two additionally important points need to be made about the use of facilitation skill in teaching cultural awareness.

### 1. Knowing all of the answers

A singular characteristic of teaching classes in prejudice, racial discrimination, and gender issues lies in the fact that there are few absolutes when it comes to dealing with attitudes. If we keep the real goal of stimulating thought and understanding in mind, rather than trying to push a specific point of view, we can at least gain some positive result. There are going to be situations during intense discussions that will necessitate us, as trainers, to say, "I can't answer that. I really don't know," or "You may have a point for discussion." This is often hard to do, especially when we usually know the answers in most of the subjects we teach. Remember, we just want to cause people to think; to re-examine their stereotypes and the way they have been socialized; and to have them understand why they may think as they do about these issues. That, in and of itself, is enough to begin change and understanding.

## 2. Being non-judgmental

Another issue to keep in mind is to be sure to treat all cultures as valuable and not hold one culture up as better than another. **All cultures are ethnocentric and have been exploitive, sexist, racist, and colonialist during periods of their existence.** Attendees can easily sense bias in an instructor and will react negatively. If people are complaining about being alienated during a session, you may want to acknowledge you're sensing that fact and ask others in the room if they are feeling the same way. A few exercises may not "click" with some groups. Asking why may leave you with some interesting outlooks on what they are thinking. Becoming defensive will only cause you to lose balance. For example, an officer may say something like, "You have been off the street too long and don't know what is going on" or "You have never worked the street. How do you know what is going on out there?" Acknowledge that it may be true, but it doesn't alter the fact that we need to learn to deal with those differences. Ask what their perceptions are as to how "working the street" has changed. You may begin an excellent discussion about the subject at hand.

Remember, you may not have to say anything about comments or responses except to acknowledge them. Much of the learning on these topics tends to occur after the attendee has left the session and has been thinking about the issues for awhile. Any changes dealing with cultural awareness are developmental and subtle and will take some time to manifest themselves into changed behaviors.

## Process Versus Content: The Importance of Dialogue

*They who only know one side of the case know little of that.*
J. Stuart Mill

Interconnected with the importance of the teaching of cultural differences in our changing communities, is understanding where the community is coming from when important issues concerning real or perceived racial discrimination come into play. As we are all aware, these issues of prejudice, bias, gender and racial discrimination are extremely emotional. Rarely can most of us restrain ourselves to deal with the logic of the situation when the rage and violence involved has offended sensibilities.

Compared to law enforcement, the general population has far more individuals who prefer deciding with social value (Feeling) rather than impersonal logic (Thinking). Couple this preference with highly charged emotional issues and logical communication becomes difficult. As is often the case when we as law enforcement professionals deal with advocate groups from the minority community, the community may make powerful assertions not necessarily based in fact, but based in social value.

This is often the case when we are dealing with advocate groups or various commissions. Representatives may make powerful assertions, for instance, that "the time for waiting is over, and the need for action is long overdue." They comment that they have suffered enough injustices to last many lifetimes. As this occurs, an interesting phenomenon is playing out. When the mind is dealing with thoughts that are extremely negative, or if the person is full of emotional rage and these feelings are not allowed out, the mind has a hard time opening itself up for other ideas or for constructive discourse. This means that people, particularly those that are or feel aggrieved, need to be able to express themselves. Understanding this is important for two reasons, both in and out of the classroom.

Those in the minority communities need to be heard. Many of their members are feeling real rage at real or perceived injustices. Dialogue must be allowed to happen, and the comments of these individuals, no matter how illogical, emotional, or off base they may sound to us, need to be heard. Even though their demands may seem inappropriate or impossible to meet, we all need to understand that they must be listened to and taken seriously. If the demands or solutions are impossible to meet, they will fall of their own weight anyway, but if they are not allowed to be placed on the table, they will fester and serve as a barrier to real discussions. People have honest, real concerns along with a sense of self tied up in many of these issues. If they are given the respect of a forum with which to express themselves, they often will move from what we perceive as emotion to more of a problem solving dialogue. Usually, if you fail to give them that opportunity or even the respect of a comment, you can expect no real movement toward solutions.

The same is appropriate for an instructor dealing with these emotional issues in a class. People need to be heard. Often when you are teaching, participants may bring up contrary views, stereotypes, caustic anecdotes, and other hostile comments. Abuse may be heaped on the instructor and on the minority being discussed. What is happening is that these individuals' personal ideas and, in some cases, self-esteem are under attack. Rarely can a positive dialogue take place when this is occurring.

As people say what they feel needs to be said, they usually become aware of their own mis-statements and over-simplifications. The negative emotions, once expressed, seem to moderate.

This is called **catharsis**. Once the tension is released, often a person can see a different perspective in the situation and begins to gain additional self-insight. Gordon Allport, in his classic book *The Nature of Prejudice*, states that even though catharsis alone is not a curative, it does, however, clear out some negative emotion and allows opportunity for the other side of the issue to be heard. If the original statements regarding race, culture, or stereotyping have been exaggerated, slanted, or unfair (as they usually are), saying them out loud often results in understanding how one-sided they really are and induces a person to seek a more balanced point of view.

During these types of discussions, much emotion will be apparent. Don't lose sight of the fact that as you are hearing emotion-driven, biased, often one-sided characterizations and comments, others in the class are hearing them too. Be assured that the majority of the others hearing the comments are aware of the exaggerations and even though they may be struggling with their own personal prejudices, can often be called upon to modify the comments to be more balanced. Be sure to utilize this excellent resource by asking "How about a comment about this from other members of the class. What do the rest of you think?" It also gives you more time to reflect on your reply.

We are, by virtue of being members of this profession, problem solvers. We may find it hard to just listen for a period of time without trying to come up with solutions to the problem. We often listen briefly to the rage and emotional language being expressed by citizens who may prefer the SF or NF cognitive style of communication, coupled with being members of higher context cultures, and try to "fix" the problem. We may immediately suggest more training or more programs without allowing more dialogue to take place. If we allow a forum from which the members of the community can speak and give them the respect of listening carefully, they will move to more of a problem solving dialogue. It is critically important we understand our styles as communicators and problem solvers as well as understanding the cognitive styles and cultural context of those in our communities.

---

You have just read a book dealing with how police officers can look at the same issue in many different ways. Realizing this, there should be no doubt in your mind that you can increase the quality of your decision making just by involving your associates in that decision making process. All you need to do is just ask. With input from many points of view, you will not only be surprised at the results, but the overall benefits will be great.

The challenges of the next millennium will test us all. As leaders, we must take advantage of all of the tools available to us. Understanding the different personality types in the profession and the strengths our associates have to offer can go a long way toward benefiting our organizations. Using this knowledge to our best advantage can give us the ability to continue to move towards the many challenges yet to come.

# Appendix A:
# The Myers-Briggs Type Indicator

Katharine Briggs, an educator, became interested in similarities and differences in human personality during World War I. She began to develop her own typology, largely through the study of bibliographies. During her research, she discovered the existence of Carl Jung's theory on personality types, which she began to explore and elaborate on.

Katharine was married to Lyman Briggs, a versatile scientist, who was the director of the National Bureau of Standards. He was a forerunner in the development of modern aviation and atomic energy, in addition to being an explorer of the stratosphere and the continent of Antarctica. They had one child, Isabel, who entered Swarthmore College at age 16 and graduated first in her class in 1919. Having long been interested in her mother's work in Jungian typology, she was determined to develop an instrument to make the theory of practical use.

Isabel Myers began the task of developing an item pool that would identify the different psychological types as described by Jung. For years, she researched and tested numerous students as she developed the instrument. The response to Myers' efforts from organized psychology was cool, if not hostile. The measurement of personality was considered a dubious enterprise by many psychologists, and among those few who were interested in personality theory and measurement, typologies were not in good repute. Trait and factor scales were the focus of research, and Myers' lack of established credentials (she was not a psychologist) didn't help to contribute to the acceptance of the Myers-Briggs Type Indicator (MBTI).

Myers' work did attract attention from a few assessment experts. Henry Chauncey, director of the Educational Testing Service, was sufficiently impressed with the instrument to approach Myers and offer to distribute the test for research purposes, which was done in 1962. During the next decade, several well known psychologists and researchers began using the instrument and writing about it. In 1975, publication of the MBTI was transferred to Consulting Psychologists Press, Palo Alto, California, to allow more widespread use. Also, in 1975, the Center for Applications of Psychological Type was founded in Gainesville, Florida, by Mary McCaulley, Ph.D., and Isabel Myers, as a research laboratory for the Indicator.

## The Design of The Myers-Briggs Type Indicator

The MBTI is probably the most widely used psychological instrument for team building and communications training in organizations today. In individual or group sessions, people can gain real insight into the ways individuals naturally look at issues from completely different points of view.

The instrument is exceptionally well researched, valid, reliable, and is non-judgmental in nature. It is intended for use with normal, healthy people. The instrument is based on rich theory and is used internationally. As a matter of fact, the instrument is presently being translated into numerous other languages. Jung's theory on psychological types is generally assumed to transcend races, sexes, and cultures as it deals with *the behavior of the human mind*.

The MBTI is a forced choice, self-disclosure instrument used to implement Jung's theory of type, intended for determining basic preferences among normal personalities. It comes in several forms, including Form F, Form G, an abbreviated Form G, and Form M. The various forms of the MBTI are Class B psychological instruments and can be administered by persons who have training in their use and have met the professional qualifications required.

The instrument measures preferences on four main dichotomies which are: Extraversion or Introversion, Sensing or Intuition, Thinking or Feeling, and Judging or Perceiving. Even though the contents of this book only concentrate on Jungian cognitive styles, or functions, Jung discussed Extraversion and Introversion at great length. In understanding the theory and the effect they have on communication, the following is noted:

**Extraversion and Introversion**

When we talk about Introverts and Extraverts in Jungian typology we are not talking about sociability. I know many Introverts that are very social and many Extraverts that are relatively quiet individuals. The director of training for a large police organization was a strong Introvert as measured by the MBTI, and he extraverted all day as an instructor and manager. He did, however, prefer to conceptualize internally by himself rather than externally with his staff.

Because the main focus of my book was to look at the way various officers differed in the way they took in information and made decisions, I did not specifically look at the interaction of Extraversion or Introversion. I interacted with both Extraverts and Introverts, but was more concerned with the way they communicated their ideas about their occupation, the words and descriptions used, than in the way they formulated the ideas, externally or internally. If they introverted the ideas (processed them internally without immediately commenting about the subject of the question), I would just wait as they thought about the question and then responded. With the Extraverts, I would just banter back and forth as they formulated the ideas verbally until they had come to a firm conclusion.

June Singer, a Jungian psychologist, studied Jung's work extensively and in her 1973 book *Boundaries of the Soul* stated that Jung described the Introvert as one who perceives in symbolic forms and is directed primarily toward internally understanding what is seen. The Introvert's interest in self-knowledge prevents him or her from being overpowered by the influence of outside, subjective surroundings. The Introvert deals with internal thoughts and concepts and defends against external intrusions. Introverts set themselves and the subjective psychic process above achievement in the public domain.

The Extravert, conversely, seeks meaning and expression outside. An object, external to oneself, appeals intrinsically to the Extravert and captures the focus of interest. As a result, the Extravert has a tendency to abandon concern for self to concern for others. The Extravert is more socially oriented and seeks recognition from others as a predominant value.

For Extraverts, the dominant process habitually monitors the outer world of people and things, while the auxiliary process involves the inner world of concepts and ideas. For Introverts, on the other hand, Extraversion must be accommodated to a considerable extent whether they want it or not. Paralleling the Extraverts, the Introvert's dominant process dwells in the inner realm while Extraversion is left to the auxiliary. But if the Introvert's auxiliary process is not adequately developed, the outward behaviors and interactions of the Introvert will appear very awkward, accidental, and often uncomfortable.

The issue of dominant and auxiliary processes creates an interesting twist in how Introverts are perceived by others. When dealing with an Extravert, the dominant process, inasmuch as it is Extraverted, is visible and conspicuous. As an example, when an Extravert is asked a question, they will usually respond immediately, as they prefer to use their Extraversion in the process. As they talk, they are thinking through the answer so they may appear to change their minds as they go through the process. Their most trusted, most mature way of using their minds is immediately apparent. With Introverts, the reverse is true. Their dominant process is not readily apparent, since they are communicating with the outside world through their auxiliary. They will conceptualize in their minds before speaking and that is why they may appear to be more "quiet" or "deliberate."

## Judging and Perceiving

The other attitudes that Isabel Myers and her mother Katharine Briggs measured were Perception and Judgment, believing people showed a preference for taking in information more than making a decision or vice versa. This was an extension of Jung's theory and actually was the key to making the theory workable and understandable.

People who prefer to take in information rather than make a decision tend to be more curious, flexible, tolerant, and look at time in a different way. They like to experience new things and do not enjoy regimentation. They are the ones that are usually late to meetings by several minutes and seemed rushed to take in information. On the other hand, those who prefer to make a decision rather than take in information enjoy being decisive, structured, planned, and settled. They like to have closure on issues. They will meet deadlines in advance and can seem driven by the clock.

We have now covered all four of the polarities measured by the MBTI. These are illustrated in more detail on Table 1. This table includes both the attitudes (EI, JP) and the functions (SN, TF). In this book, my focus has been on the functions, also called the cognitive styles, not on the attitudes.

### Table 4: Four Principle Psychological Polarities

|  | Preference for | A Person focuses on |
|---|---|---|
| E-I | E: Extraversion<br>I: Introversion | The outer world of personal interaction<br>The inner world of concepts and ideas |
| S-N | S: Sensing<br>N: Intuition | Practical and factual details<br>Patterns and meanings |
| T-F | T: Thinking<br>F: Feeling | Using logical, impersonal analysis<br>Weighing human values and motives |
| J-P | J: Judgment<br>P: Perception | Closure and structure<br>Flexibility and openness |

Table 5 illustrates the various combinations of preferences which constitute the sixteen personality types. Everyone is an individual, but shares various characteristics with others of the same type. People tend to act in ways that are most comfortable to them, which may or may not be the same as the ways others approach problems or situations. When this occurs, knowing about the different ways people function will go a long way in giving us insight to maintain good working relationships with others. It is also useful to recognize differences in various preferred ways of functioning that those in other occupations may use. We as law enforcement administrators can benefit by understanding the ways people, inside and outside our organization, prefer to take in information and make decisions as we deal with them on a daily basis.

The descriptors on Table 5 are from Sandra Hirsh and Jean Kummerow's *Introduction to Type in Organizations* (1987, 1990). Isabel Myers designed the type table in a certain pattern, which is followed here. The table is divided into various columns linking like types together. The Thinking types are in the outside columns, the Feeling types in the inside columns. The table is split with the upper eight types being Introverts and the lower eight types being Extraverts. The Sensing types occupy the right two columns and the Intuitive types occupy the left two columns. The Judging types occupy the top and bottom rows with the Perceptive types in the middle.

## Table 5: Descriptors of Type Characteristics

| Sensing Types | | Intuitive Types | |
|---|---|---|---|
| **Thinking** | **Feeling** | **Feeling** | **Thinking** |
| **ISTJ** | **ISFJ** | **INFJ** | **INTJ** |
| factual | detailed | committed | independent |
| through | traditional | loyal | logical |
| systematic | patient | creative | original |
| dependable | practical | intense | visionary |
| realistic | organized | conceptual | theoretical |
| sensible | protective | sensitive | demanding |
| **ISTP** | **ISFP** | **INFP** | **INTP** |
| logical | caring | gentle | logical |
| realistic | sensitive | adaptable | cognitive |
| factual | observant | committed | detached |
| analytical | cooperative | creative | reserved |
| applied | loyal | devoted | precise |
| adaptable | trusting | empathetic | speculative |
| **ESTP** | **ESFP** | **ENFP** | **ENTP** |
| adaptable | enthusiastic | creative | enterprising |
| versatile | adaptable | curious | independent |
| energetic | friendly | versatile | strategic |
| alert | talkative | expressive | adaptable |
| pragmatic | cooperative | perceptive | resourceful |
| persuasive | outgoing | friendly | clever |
| **ESTJ** | **ESFJ** | **ENFJ** | **ENTJ** |
| logical | loyal | idealistic | logical |
| decisive | sociable | personable | decisive |
| direct | thorough | enthusiastic | strategic |
| practical | tactful | expressive | controlled |
| impersonal | responsive | diplomatic | challenging |
| structured | sympathetic | congenial | objective |

Adapted from *Introduction to Type in Organizations* by Sandra K. Hirsh and Jean M. Kummerow. Palo Alto, CA: Consulting Psychologists Press, 1987, 1990. Used with permission. Further reproduction is prohibited without publisher's written consent.

## MBTI Cognitive Styles

Carl Jung felt that the center of our personality and how we are, was determined, to a large extent, by how we take in information and how we make decisions. He called these the "functions." The Perceptive functions are Sensing and Intuition, and the Judging functions are Thinking and Feeling.

The four functions combine in patterns we call the cognitive styles. With one letter from the SN dichotomy and the other letter from the TF dichotomy, these cognitive styles are ST, SF, NF, and NT. As you can see on Table 5, the four columns are arranged by cognitive style in this order. For example, the types with the cognitive style of ST (Sensing Thinking) are listed in the far left hand column: ISTJ, ISTP, ESTP, and ESTJ. The SF cognitive style is shared by the types in the next column to the right: ISFJ, ISFP, ESFP, and ESFJ. Those with the NF cognitive style are grouped in the third column from the left: INFJ, INFP, ENFP, and ENFJ. In the far right column we have the four types with the NT cognitive style: INTJ, INTP, ENTP, and ENTJ.

The cognitive styles of ST, SF, NF, and NT fit well with current cognitive psychology. Personality researchers recognize Jung's theory and the MBTI as cognitive style approaches. Mary McCaulley, a founder of the Center for Applications of Psychological Type, has stated the foundation of type theory rests on the ways people take in information and make decisions, hence the core of the Jung/MBTI approach is the cognitive process. The information, comments, and research contained in this book are all based on the MBTI cognitive styles.

# Appendix B:
# Police Personality Research

Concern with the quality of American policing and police dates back roughly to 1931 and the publication of the findings of the Wickersham Commission. This commission produced the first systematic explanation of the American criminal justice system. While the explanation centered on routine police practices, the report encouraged further research by people who today would call themselves criminologists.

The concerns and research seemed to focus on what makes up a law enforcement officer; and in knowing how the officer may function, how can we better understand and direct police behavior? Scholars started to gather data, and gather they did! In the late 1950s through the early 1960s, numerous studies were conducted in the profession. Peter Manning, a criminologist and researcher, listed over 78 various police research projects being conducted in 1976 alone, the era considered as the "Golden Age of Police Research." It was interesting to note, however, that research on police personality involving the use of the Myers-Briggs Type Indicator didn't surface until 1978.

Wayne B. Hanewicz was the first major researcher to publish using the Jungian conceptual framework of personality types for the law enforcement profession. He used the MBTI framework to categorize various traits displayed by police officers into the sixteen types defined by the Myers-Briggs Type Indicator. Hanewicz defined personality according to sociologist Thomas C. Gray's (1975) notion of affinity: "...a predisposition to adhere partially to a set of distinctive sentiments that can be expanded and reinforced by training and socialization."

Hanewicz interpreted previous research as reflecting two major positions: first, the police personalty is something police possess by virtue of being police, (i.e., job related) and, secondly, the police personality is something inherent in people who choose to become police officers. In the first case, "police personality" refers to a group of traits that are acquired after employment and is characteristic of the police profession alone. In the second case, "police personality" signifies a group of traits common to, but not exclusive of, police officers. Using this definition, a person who enters the police profession may share common characteristics with a person who enters another field which stresses some of the same traits needed to do police work.

Many researchers felt there was a personality exclusive to police, but Hanewicz disagreed, taking into consideration the Myers-Briggs instrument, Carl Jung's theory, and other studies. Hanewicz and others felt there were possible overlaps between the personality required for police work and some other jobs.

According to Hanewicz, Jungian typology represented a promising approach to investigating the commonalities between police work and other occupations. He described a study undertaken with the Miami, Florida, police department in an attempt to improve police-citizen interaction. Determinants of police behavior were studied to understand the factors which influence police behavior and to relate them to police functions.

In the study, psychiatrist Jesse Rubin is quoted as saying, "The type of people who enter police work are generally psychologically healthy and competent young men who display common personality features that should serve them well in a police career." He described them as generally restless and assertive, with a high level of physical energy. Further, their restlessness seems to derive from an aversion to introspection; rather, "policemen look to the environment for perceptual stimulation in order to maintain alertness and optimal functioning."

Hanewicz also quoted a study of the New York City Police Department training activities, funded by the National Institute of Law Enforcement and Criminal Justice, which compared the value dimensions of police recruits entering the department in 1959 and again in 1968. He found a remarkable similarity among the personality traits valued by the recruits in both years, even though they were a decade apart. Alertness, job knowledge, honesty, dedication, and common sense were the top five of forty possible choices in the 1959 group, and were among the top six in the 1968 group.

Hanewicz's conclusions concentrated primarily on the predominance of certain personalty styles in the police profession and the fact these personality traits were shared by police along with those in certain other occupations. However, he only touched on the various possible organizational implications Jungian typology suggests in better understanding the law enforcement profession.

In the 1980s several other researchers also examined police personality through the use of the MBTI. Ron Cacioppe and Philip Mock, two researchers from Australia, conducted a study on police self-actualization, quality of work experience, and stress. The personality type distribution in their sample of 191 senior Australian police resembled that of Hanewicz.

Another researcher, Ronald Lynch, who was with the Institute of Government at the University of North Carolina, conducted several studies involving the use of the Myers-Briggs Type Indicator. Lynch found the distribution of the various Jungian types throughout the police profession was much the same as the distribution Hanewicz found. Lynch also commented on the fact that the tasks of policing were also common to other occupations as well, such as banking and engineering.

Hobart M. Henson, a Deputy Director with the Illinois State Police, conducted a comprehensive study utilizing the MBTI, seeking to develop criteria to help in recruiting persons especially suited to be police officers and to more effectively select, train, motivate, and plan for growth in his agency. His data, drawn from a comprehensive sample of 2,114 veteran and recruit police officers, indicated the same general distribution of personality types according to the MBTI as did Hanewicz and Lynch.

I combined the type distributions from the studies of Wayne Hanewicz, Hobart Henson, and Ron Lynch, along with the study I conducted with three hundred police executives, and came up with a Composite Police Profile according to Myers-Briggs cognitive styles. As one can see from Table 6, the Intuitive Feeling (NF) cognitive style is least represented in law enforcement. The majority of police personnel clearly prefer the Sensing Thinking (ST) cognitive style.

### Table 6: Composite Police Profile
### N = 3,001

| MBTI Norms U.S. Percentages* | | Composite Police Mean Percentages | |
|---|---|---|---|
| NF | 15-21% | NF | 5 |
| SF | 31-41% | SF | 11 |
| NT | 15-22% | NT | 14 |
| ST | 32-42% | ST | 70 |

From *Estimated Frequencies of the Types in the United States Population* by C. R. Martin, 1996. Gainesville, FL: Center for Applications of Psychological Type. Used by permission.

Note that about 50 percent of the individuals who make up MBTI norms prefer making decisions (Judgment) with the use of the Feeling function, while only 20 percent of the police prefer making decisions in that manner.

# Appendix C: Personality Types in Other Professions

The Center for Applications of Psychological Type (CAPT), a research center in Gainesville, Florida, founded by Isabel Myers and Mary McCaulley, maintains a data bank containing MBTI results from over 600,000 individuals. The data shows that certain psychological types are attracted to various occupations disproportionately to the distribution of types in the general population. This is why people in various occupations tend to resemble each other in the way they take in information and make decisions. This data bank is being added to daily by those individuals who use the Myers-Briggs Type Indicator.

There have not been any formal studies conducted with the expressed purpose in mind of determining a more exact estimate of the type distribution in the United States lately. The estimates in the following examples are the result of taking the numerous samples of those instruments on file at CAPT and extrapolating the following results.

Table 7 estimates percentages of various personality types in the general population in the United States.

### Table 7: Estimated Distribution in United States by Psychological Preferences

| | |
|---|---|
| Extraversion | 50-55% |
| Introversion | 45-50% |
| | |
| Sensing | 65-70% |
| Intuition | 30-35% |
| | |
| Thinking | 65-70% males, 35-40% females |
| Feeling. | 35-40% males, 60-65% females |
| | |
| Judgment | 55-60% |
| Perception | 40-45% |

From *Estimated Frequencies of the Types in the United States Population* by C. R. Martin. Copyright 1996 Center for Applications of Psychological Type. Used by permission.

This estimate was compiled by the Center for Applications of Psychological Type in late 1996 using the results of several major studies deemed to be generally representative of the general U.S. population. It includes the results of Myers' sample of 12,860 males and 20,006 females, all of whom were eleventh and twelfth grade students from Pennsylvania; cases from the CAPT data bank scored from 1978 to 1982; SRI International's Values and Lifestyles Program samples; and Hammer and Mitchell's national stratified sample collected from 1988 to 1991. It is interesting to note, however, that samples from individuals in various other cultures such as Japanese middle managers, Canadian consultants, Australian police officers, and English managers, when compared to their counterparts in the United States, generally reflect the same type distributions throughout the sixteen personality types.

The utility of population norms for researchers is for comparison of the distribution of types among different occupations. These differences can serve as a foundation for understanding the relationship between personality type and occupations.

### Table 8: Estimated Distribution in United States by Cognitive Style

| | | |
|---|---|---|
| Sensing Thinking | ST | 32-42% |
| Sensing Feeling | SF | 31-41% |
| Intuitive Feeling | NF | 15-21% |
| Intuitive Thinking | NT | 15-22% |

From *Estimated Frequencies of the Types in the United States Population* by C. R. Martin. Copyright 1996 Center for Applications of Psychological Type. Used by permission.

## Cognitive Style Preferences in Various Occupations

To illustrate that the distribution of cognitive styles can differ considerably from one occupation to another, I looked at four occupations outside the police profession that call for the use of different talents to perform the various job functions.

### Table 9: Managerial and Professional Bank Employees
### N = 110

| | | Percent | Number |
|---|---|---|---|
| Sensing Thinking | ST | 57.90 | 65 |
| Sensing Feeling | SF | 27.10 | 29 |
| Intuitive Feeling | NF | 7.50 | 8 |
| Intuitive Thinking | NT | 7.58 | 8 |
| Totals | | 100.00 | 110 |

Data from *Atlas of Type Tables* by G. P. Macdaid, M. H. McCaulley, and R. I. Kainz, 1986. Gainesville, FL: Center for Applications of Psychological Type. Used by permission.

## Bank Employees

Occupational tasks in the banking industry include those of counting money, balancing accounts at the end of each day, and keeping ledgers, among others. Additional daily tasks involved are computer operations, data typing, use of electronic posting machines, the need to write legibly, do simple mathematical tasks, and other repetitive jobs. These tasks tend to focus on the immediate experience and require realism, acute powers of observation, memory, ability to deal with detail, and practicality, which is appropriate for those persons oriented toward the Sensing function. The tasks further reflect the need for analytical ability, critical and logical thinking, characteristics of those preferring the Thinking function of decision making.

As depicted in Table 9, the Sensing Thinking style is over-represented in this occupational group (57.90%) compared to the general population estimates (32%-42%) with the least represented groups being Intuitive Feeling and Intuitive Thinking. The job tasks in this industry would seem to include a majority of Sensing tasks, which are grounded in the present. The Sensing Feeling group with 27.10% is only slightly under-represented compared to the general population estimate of 31%-41% for this preference. These SFs may most likely be those persons involved in the public relations tasks of tellers and loan officers. Additionally, many deal with tasks using the five senses such as counting money, balancing ledgers, and working with figures.

## Small Business Managers

The second group, represented in Table 10, the small business managers, reflects an even higher ST preference (70.6%). The NF percentage of 3.33% is greatly under-represented when compared to the general population (15%-21%). Small business managers are involved in investigating and diagnosing problems using logical, analytical thinking in order to reach practical, sound conclusions. Logical thinking is essential when laying the groundwork. Interestingly, research has shown that one of the greatest causes for managerial failure is the inability to get along with others. This makes sense if one considers the under-representation of Feeling types (18.66%) compared to the general population norm of 46%-62%.

### Table 10: Small Business Managers
### N = 150

|  |  | Percent | Number |
|---|---|---|---|
| Sensing Thinking | ST | 70.67 | 106 |
| Sensing Feeling | SF | 15.33 | 23 |
| Intuitive Feeling | NF | 3.33 | 5 |
| Intuitive Thinking | NT | 10.67 | 10 |
| Totals |  | 100.00 | 150 |

Data from *Atlas of Type Tables* by G. P. Macdaid, M. H. McCaulley, and R. I. Kainz, 1986. Gainesville, FL: Center for Applications of Psychological Type. Used by permission.

## Roman Catholic Religious Order Members

Table 11 reflects the MBTI preferences of members of Roman Catholic Religious Orders. The ST function in this occupation is 10.64%, with the NF preference at 32.87%, almost the reverse of the occupations of banking and small business managers. The NF style, which is the dominant function in this sample, reflects the strengths of harmony, feeling, compassion, love, loyalty, and human insight. The occupations involving religious service generally would seem to call for unselfish concern, deference to others, maturity of spirit, and a calling to help others.

### Table 11: Roman Catholic Religious Order Members
### N = 2,002

|  |  | Percent | Number |
|---|---|---|---|
| Sensing Thinking | ST | 10.64 | 213 |
| Sensing Feeling | SF | 49.45 | 990 |
| Intuitive Feeling | NF | 32.87 | 658 |
| Intuitive Thinking | NT | 7.04 | 141 |
| Totals |  | 100.00 | 2,002 |

Data from *Atlas of Type Tables* by G. P. Macdaid, M. H. McCaulley, and R. I. Kainz, 1986. Gainesville, FL: Center for Applications of Psychological Type. Used by permission.

## Psychologists

Members of the fourth occupational group are represented in Table 12. The occupation of psychology deals with understanding human behavior, solutions to problems in human relations, and assisting with personal adjustment. The locations of the work sites, e.g., medical professions, academic institutions, and various types of private counseling contexts, however, constitutes a wide continuum.

Medical and counseling psychologists, for example, focus on healing the human psyche. Industrial psychologists concentrate on trying to make the work place better for people. Conceivably, if one were to study this group in more depth, the majority of Intuitive Feeling types in this profession would probably be those who operate as clinicians in these contexts.

|                   | Table 12: Psychologists<br>N = 289 |         |        |
|-------------------|------|---------|--------|
|                   |      | Percent | Number |
| Sensing Thinking  | ST   | 11.07   | 32     |
| Sensing Feeling   | SF   | 8.30    | 24     |
| Intuitive Feeling | NF   | 49.83   | 144    |
| Intuitive Thinking| NT   | 30.80   | 89     |
| Totals            |      | 100.00  | 289    |

Data from *Atlas of Type Tables* by G. P. Macdaid, M. H. McCaulley, and R. I. Kainz, 1986. Gainesville, FL: Center for Applications of Psychological Type. Used by permission.

On the other hand, those who conduct research in either medical or academic settings may account for the Intuitive Thinkers among psychologists. Certainly the types of training and skills they need in order to conduct experiments, analyze them, and write up the results, emphasize the rational synthesis of information characteristic of the preference for Intuitive Thinking.

As you can clearly see, various individuals exhibiting specific cognitive styles congregate in certain occupations, whose specific tasks call upon certain skills. People are obviously individuals and all types are represented in all occupations; however, by looking at the majority of cognitive styles in any one occupation, you can make an educated guess at the skills required for that occupation.

### Uncommon Cognitive Styles

Even though the majority of people in one occupation share the same cognitive styles, you can find others in the occupation who are very successful, but don't share the cognitive styles of the majority. These are the persons we call the **uncommon types or uncommon cognitive styles** in a occupation. These are the officers referred to as "a couple of degrees of true north" or, as one officer called himself "a cigar store Indian." Knowing how these people function becomes more and more important as we try to make decisions about work and the people who perform in our organizations. Knowing how the majority of people in law enforcement function, along with these "deviations from true north," becomes more and more important as our tasks become more specialized.

# References

Cacioppe, Ron L., and Mock, Philip (1985). Developing the police officer at work. *Leadership and Organizational Development Journal, 6,* 5.

Frisbee, George R. (1988). Cognitive styles: An alternative to Keirsey's temperaments. *Journal of Psychological Type, 16,* 13- 21.

Gray, Thomas C. (1975). Selecting for a police subculture. In Jerome H. Skolnick and Thomas C. Gray (Eds.), *Police in America*. Boston, MA: Educational Associates.

Goldstein, Herman (1977). *Policing a free society*. Cambridge, MA: Ballinger Publishing.

Hanewicz, Wayne B. (1978, April). Police personality: A Jungian perspective. *Crime and Delinquency, 24,* 2, 152-172.

Hennessy, Stephen M. (1992). A study of uncommon Myers-Briggs cognitive styles in law enforcement (Doctoral dissertation, University of St. Thomas, St. Paul, 1990). *Dissertation Abstracts International*, 52/12, 4308A. (University Microfilms No. AAC92-11842).

Hennessy, Stephen M. (1997, December). Multicultural awareness training structure with Arizona police recruits. *Crime & Justice International,* 9-11.

Hennessy, Stephen M., Warring, D. F., Arnott, J. S., Cornett-DeVito, M. M., & Heuett, G. H. (1998). *A cultural awareness trainer's manual for law enforcement officers.* Scottsdale, AZ: Leadership Inc.

Henson, Hobart M. (1984). *A study in police personality in a major police organization.* Unpublished study of the Illinois State Police, Springfield, Illinois.

Hirsh, Sandra, and Kummerow, Jean (1987). *Introduction to type in organizations.* Palo Alto, CA: Consulting Psychologists Press.

Jung, Carl G. (1974). *Psychological types* (R.F.C. Hull Translation). Zurich: Rascher Verlag (Original work published 1921).

Kummerow, Jean M. (1988). A methodology for verifying type: Research results. *Journal of Psychological Type, 15,* 20-25.

Lynch, Ronald G. (1986). *The police manager.* New York, NY: Random House.

Manning, Peter (1976). The researcher: An alien in the police world. In Arthur Neiderhoffer and Abraham S. Blumberg (Eds.), *The ambivalent force.* Hinsdale, IL: The Dryden Press.

Macdaid, Gerald P., McCaulley, Mary H., & Kainz, Richard I. (1986). *Atlas of type tables.* Gainesville, FL: Center for Applications of Psychological Type.

McCaulley, Mary H. (1990). The Myers-Briggs Type Indicator and leadership. In K. E. Clark and M. B. Clark (Eds.), *Measures of leadership*. West Orange, NJ: Leadership Library of America, Inc.

Martin, Charles R. (1996). *Estimated frequencies of the types in the United States population*. Gainesville, FL: Center for Applications of Psychological Type.

Myers, Isabel Briggs (1976). *Myers-Briggs Type Indicator, Form G*. Palo Alto, CA: Consulting Psychologists Press.

Myers, Isabel Briggs, and McCaulley, Mary H. (1985). *Manual: A guide to the development and use of the Myers-Briggs Type Indicator*. Palo Alto, CA: Consulting Psychologists Press.

Rubin, Jesse G. (1974). Police identity and the police role. In Jack Goldsmith and Sharon S. Goldsmith (Eds.), *The police community: Dimensions of an occupational subculture*. Pacific Palisades, CA: Palisades Publishing.

Sanders, Charles B., Jr. (1970). *Police education and training: Key to better law enforcement*. Washington, DC: Brookings Institute.

Singer, June (1973). *Boundaries of the soul: A primer of Jung's psychology*. Garden City, NY: Anchor Press.

Wilson, James Q. (1985). *Thinking about crime*. New York, NY: Vantage Books.

# About the Author

Stephen M. Hennessy, born on the Iron Range in Minnesota, began his law enforcement career in 1966 as a Special Agent of the Federal Bureau of Investigation and served in both Houston, Texas, and Newark, New Jersey. Steve returned home to Minnesota in 1973 and joined the Minnesota Department of Public Safety serving as Director of the Cooperative Area Narcotics Squad until 1977, when he was appointed Deputy Superintendent in charge of investigations for the Criminal Apprehension Division. In 1984, he became responsible for the laboratory, information systems, finance, budget, and planning of the division until his retirement in 1991. He presently serves as the Training Administrator for the Phoenix, Arizona Police Department.

Steve holds a Bachelor of Science in Business Administration from the University of Denver, a Master's Degree in Public Safety Education and Administration, and a Doctorate in Educational Leadership from the University of St. Thomas in St. Paul, Minnesota. He is the lead author of *A Cultural Awareness Trainer's Manual for Law Enforcement*, a contributing author to *Multicultural Perspectives in Criminal Justice*, and has authored numerous articles on cultural awareness training. He is an associate faculty member of Arizona State University teaching in the

School of Public Affairs, and with Northern Arizona University in the Master's in Educational Leadership program. He instructs for the International Association of Chiefs of Police in the cultural awareness and leadership fields.

Dr. Hennessy speaks and consults on the subjects of leadership, type, and cultural awareness in the law enforcement profession. He may be contacted at Leadership Inc., of Scottsdale, 7418 E. Helm Drive, Scottsdale, AZ 85260. Tel. (602) 443-2737, fax (602) 391-1903.

71 — STS

103 — Edward T. Hall (Sociologist & expert in communication) — [Context]

104 — rational OR *personal* solutions.

124 — Increasing the quality of your decision making by involving your associates in the process —